THE FAMILY CREATIVE WORKSHOP

11

Music Making
Napkin Folding, Neckties, Needlepoint
Oil Painting, Ojo de Dios
Organic Gardening
Origami, Papermaking, Papier Mâché

Plenary Publications International, Inc.
New York and Amsterdam

Published by Plenary Publications
International, Incorporated
300 East 40 Street, New York, N. Y.
10016, for the Blue Mountain
Crafts Council.

Library of Congress Catalog Card
Number: 73–89331.
Complete set International Standard
Book Number: 0–88459–021–6.
Volume 11 International Standard
Book Number: 0–88459–010–0.

Manufactured in the United States
of America. Printed and bound
by the W. A. Krueger Company,
Brookfield, Wisconsin.

Printing preparation
by Lanman Lithoplate Company.

Publishers:
Plenary Publications
International, Incorporated
300 East 40 Street
New York, New York 10016

Originating editor of the series:
Allen Davenport Bragdon

Nancy Jackson
ADMINISTRATIVE ASSISTANT

Jerry Curcio
PRODUCTION MANAGER

Editorial preparation:
Tree Communications, Inc.
250 Park Avenue South
New York, New York 10003

Rodney Friedman
EDITORIAL DIRECTOR

Ronald Gross
DESIGN DIRECTOR

Paul Levin
DIRECTOR OF PHOTOGRAPHY

Donal Dinwiddie
CONSULTING EDITOR

Jill Munves
TEXT EDITOR

Sonja Douglas
ART DIRECTOR

Rochelle Lapidus
DESIGNER

Lucille O'Brien
EDITORIAL PRODUCTION

Ruth Forst Michel
Barnet Friedman
COPYREADERS

Eva Gold
ADMINISTRATIVE MANAGER

Editors for this volume:
Andrea DiNoto
MUSIC-MAKING

Linda Hetzer
NAPKIN FOLDING
NEEDLEPOINT
OJO DE DIOS

Nancy Bruning Levine
ORIGAMI
PAPIER-MÂCHÉ

Marilyn Nierenberg
OIL PAINTING

Marilyn Ratner
NECKTIES

Mary Grace Skurka
ORGANIC GARDENING
PAPERMAKING

Contributing Illustrators:
Marina Givotovsky
Lynn Matus
Kevin Maher
Sally Shimizu

Production:
Thom Augusta
Marsha Gold
Amanda Lester
Nicholas Martori

Photo and illustration credits:
MUSIC MAKING: All photos by Robert Wood except pages 1286 (top left), 1287, and black and white photos on pages 1288 (top left and top center), 1290 (left), 1293, 1294 (right), 1295 (bottom right), and 1296. NAPKIN FOLDING: On page 1301, the dinnerware, Royal Worcester Strawberry Fair; the glassware, Worcester Crystal Clear; the flatware, Worcester Cumberland. All are courtesy of Royal Worcester Porcelain Co., Inc. The tablecloth and napkins are courtesy of Plummer McCutcheon at Hammacher Schlemmer. NECKTIES: Etching, page 1308, courtesy of New York Public Library Picture Collection; recycled tie skirt, page 1316, by Nancy Bruning Levine: tying a tie, page 1317, courtesy of Men's Tie Association. OIL PAINTING: Photographs on pages 1336 and 1337, courtesy of the Philadelphia Museum of Art. ORIGAMI: Tree, page 1385, courtesy of American Tree & Wreath, New York, N.Y.

The Project-Evaluation
Symbols appearing in the
title heading at the
beginning of each project
have these meanings:

Range of approximate cost:
¢ Low: under $5 or free
and found natural materials

$ Medium: about $10

$$ High: above $15

Estimated time to completion for an unskilled adult:
⌛ Hours

🕐 Days

📅 Weeks

Suggested level of experience:
Child alone

Supervised child or
family project

Unskilled adult

Specialized prior training

Tools and equipment:
Small hand tools

Large hand
and household tools

Specialized
or powered equipment

On the cover:
Mix oil paints to create a limitless rainbow of color, as described in the Oil Painting entry, beginning on page 1334 . Undiluted or thinned color can be applied to a canvas directly from the tube, with paint brushes, palette knives, rags, fingers or objects of your own invention, to produce an endless variety of textural contrasts. Photograph by Paul Levin.

Contents and Craftspeople for Volume 11:

MUSIC MAKING
Mix and Beat Well

Robert Wood is a classically trained musician and composer with more than 20 years of teaching experience in New York City schools. He travels throughout the country conducting workshops in instrument-making and setting up mini-festivals which often include his specialty —musical tree-house environments constructed from lightweight scaffolding. He has received several research grants for his experimental work in teaching music-making to beginners and is the co-author of Make Your Own Musical Instruments, *Sterling Publishing Co., N.Y.*

Imagine a free-wheeling percussion band in which the musicians are ordinary people who come and go as they please, moving from one instrument to another, picking up the beat and putting it down as the spirit moves them. Imagine these musicians finding drums, gongs, chimes, marimbas, shakers and other rhythm instruments almost asking to be played. For me, this scene is not unusual; I have arranged it in city streets, at schools, and on college campuses; for the handicapped, small children and senior citizens; at neighborhood block parties, fairs and festivals. It is a way of giving a music-making experience to everyone and anyone, particularly those who only need an excuse to discover their hidden music-making talents. But experienced musicians enjoy communal instruments too.

Festival Instruments

The good vibrations of percussion instruments have accompanied the growth of every civilization from the moment a baby first smiled at the rhythmic shaking of a rattle. Rhythm has never needed translation. Without it, you've got noise; with it, you've got music. So it is natural and logical to begin making music with percussion instruments. The idea of festival instruments—to be played spontaneously and communally—developed over the years as I worked with children, trying to create a friendly, non-competitive first experience with music-making. As it has turned out, teen-agers and adults respond just as eagerly as children to an invitation to play and share their beat with others in a public place. Of course, if you want to play more technically demanding music, you will need study and practice, but that is no reason not to have the fun of a jam session while you are learning. Usually the term "jam session" describes a group of experienced musicians improvising with each other, with each in turn showing off his skill. With communal instruments the experience can be similar, but it is more sharing than showmanship.

The instruments described here have all been devised by what I call the Festival Music Company, an organization that includes me and a volunteer staff of helpers, whose numbers vary and whose ages range from fourth graders on up.

Instrument Making

The general idea is to make each instrument so it can't be broken. Festival instruments take a beating. If they are not extra durable they will fall apart quickly during your festival since dozens of people may be pounding away on them in the course of a day. You will find that in the design of some of the instruments (see Drums, page 1289), tone quality has been sacrificed to achieve toughness. In another category I call "visual instruments," eye appeal is more important than tone (see Gongs and Chimes, page 1292). In both cases, the materials used are simple, cheap and readily available, and the examples given here have by no means exhausted the possibilities.

But this variety of materials will produce an interesting tonal mix that has a distinctive flavor. Plastic shakers (page 1288) rustle; plastic-pipe drums give a mellow thunk-thunk; wooden claves (page 1291) pepper the mix with a pleasing thock-thock-thock; wooden marimbas add a bell-like resonance; and metal gongs, while supplying tang, give a loud voice to anyone who really needs one.

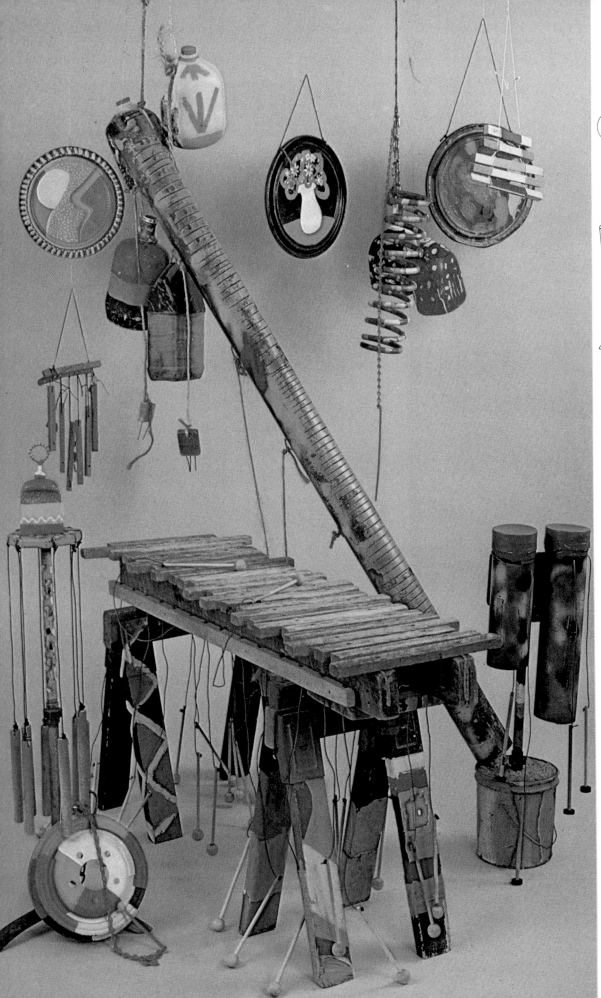

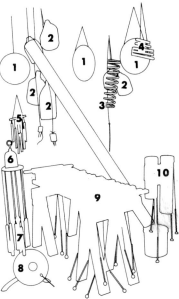

Bob Wood's primitive instruments shown at left and keyed above are some ingredients of a percussion band that anyone can make and play. The instruments are: (1) fiber-barrel-lid gongs; (2) plastic-jug shakers; (3) automobile coil-spring gong; (4) marimba a l' Africaine; (5) marimba chime; (6) tin-can bell; (7) claves (communal rhythm sticks); (8) automobile brake-drum gongs and beater; (9) communal mother marimba; (10) PVC pipe drums.

These giant pods are one kind of natural shaker. The seeds of a tropical plant, they rattle when dry.

Festival rhythm makers

Young children can begin making an instrument by eating the contents of those small plastic containers that come filled with fruit, pudding and other delicious foods. Once the container is empty and washed it can be painted in bright colors with water-based paints. It could also be sprayed a solid color first, then decorated. Partially fill such cups with anything that shakes and makes a good sound: gravel, beans, or rice, for example. A tight lid is needed since everyone likes to open a shaker to see what is inside. The lid can be cemented on with a few drops of modeling glue. These shakers make good giveaways.

Children can make shakers from small plastic food containers filled with anything that will rattle. The shaker at the left has a handle of ruffled elastic.

An artist-musician concentrates her attention on the challenge of decorating a shaker in a quiet moment before the festivities begin.

Leon proudly displays the plastic-jug shaker that he has painted with the help of his friend Delores.

A young musician keeps the beat moving with a shaker made from a plastic jug with beans inside.

These girls create their own street ballet as they dance spontaneously with their plastic shakers.

A concrete-filled pail (see Craftnotes, page 1293) supports the drummer as well as the drums it was designed to hold.

Dancing and drumming go very well together as these merry-makers demonstrate. They share a pair of plastic-pipe drums.

Age does not dim the joy of pounding out a rhythmic beat on a pair of drums.

Large shakers can be made from plastic gallon jugs with handles. These are also great fun to paint, and eventually they can be hung with other kinds of instruments. Children like to braid long ropes of colorful cloth strips or bailing cord for hanging the shakers. Like all the festival instruments, shakers will often be played in unconventional ways. I've seen players punching them back and forth and even giving them rhythmic karate kicks.

Fantastic Plastic Drums

A drum can be anything hollow and resonant that produces a tone when struck. The most primitive drums were hollowed-out tree trunks that were beaten with clubs. A membrane drum, most commonly used today, has a skin stretched across the cavity; this is struck with hands or beaters, depending upon the sound desired.

The bodies of our festival drums, pictured above, are cut from 6-foot lengths of 4-inch plastic PVC pipe, available at hardware stores, plumbing supply stores, or lumber yards. You can cut the pipe easily with an ordinary cross-cut handsaw. In any tubular instrument, a longer length produces a deeper tone and vice versa. But if you cut a piece too long, you will find the drum lacks a solid fundamental tone. A short piece, on the other hand, may give you such a thin tone you will find it unsatisfactory and discard it.

Tone also depends a great deal on the type of head used. Animal skins give a wonderful sound but are fragile and difficult to attach. A tougher material, and the best substitute I have found, is an inexpensive plastic industrial item called a 4-inch thread protector cap, available at plumbing supply stores. These fit the PVC-pipe drums almost perfectly. Used caps can sometimes be salvaged at construction sites where they are discarded.

After you press the cap down on the pipe, secure it all around with plenty of masking tape, overlapping generously. This completes the basic drum. You can paint and decorate it, attach beaters (Figure A), and mount the drum on a stand (see Craftnotes, page 1293).

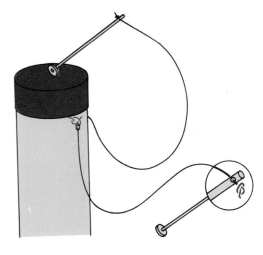

A
Figure A: To attach beaters to a drum, drill holes in the drum shell and thread lengths of cord—knotted on one end—from the inside out. The beaters are wooden dowels with rubber tips made from either small rubber balls or discs that can be found in hardware stores. Thread cords through holes in the dowels and secure knots by dipping them in glue.

Drum Beaters

Several beaters attached to each drum make the instrument communal, that is, available for many people to play at one time. Beaters, I have found, also attract souvenir hunters; so they must be fastened on securely. I use plastic-coated electrical household wire which I carefully split in half lengthwise without exposing the copper core; then I use each coated wire as ordinary cord. When tightly knotted, the cord is not easily cut or pulled off and does not wear out.

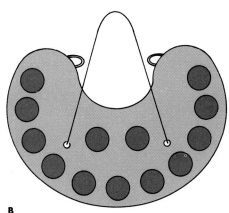

Figure B: When drums of varying lengths are mounted in holes in a thin wooden pallet, they are called demo drums and can be worn around the neck and played by one strong person.

Claves—or rhythm sticks—make the desired resonant sound when the lower stick, balanced on the fingertips of one hand, is tapped with the other.

Rubber-tipped beaters produce the best tone on plastic-pipe drums. A rubber tip bounces off the surface and helps the amateur play faster than he otherwise could. Make the handles from 9-inch lengths of dowel, 5/16 to 3/8 inch in diameter. You can improvise rubber heads from small rubber balls or hardware or plumbing items such as flat rubber discs. But gluing wood to rubber is surprisingly difficult; contact cement is the best adhesive I have found for this job. If you are making a lot of beaters at one time, punch holes in a cardboard box to hold the dowels; then apply adhesive and tips assembly-line style. When the glue is set, use a staple gun to drive a 1/4-inch staple so that one leg goes into the beater and the other into the rubber. This makes the joint additionally secure.

Attach the cord to the drum before you tie the beater to it. Cut a length about 26 inches long. In each drum, drill two holes slightly larger than the cord and about an inch apart, just below the masking tape. Knot one end of the cord and thread it from the inside of the drum shell out (Figure A). Using the same bit, drill a hole in the handle of the beater, opposite the tip. Pass the cord through this hole and knot it. Knots can be made extra secure by dipping them in glue.

When several pipe drums of varying lengths are clustered together, they are more fun to play and more interesting tonally for both player and listener. Two tones are better than one and three are better than two. The two-drum cluster (page 1289) has a pipe mount with a tripod base. You can bolt drums onto a piece of ¾-inch plywood; then attach the plywood to a pipe mount with a metal strip, as shown in the Craftnotes, page 1293.

Another cluster possibility is illustrated in Figure B, showing how thirteen drums can be mounted on a pallet and hung from the shoulders of a single player. Wide straps distribute the substantial weight, but you might add the drums one at a time as the player supports them to determine how many he can comfortably carry. These are called demo drums; they suit a wandering minstrel given the job of summoning people to the festival. Other festival instruments, too, like the marimba, can grow from the simplest solo instrument (page 1294) into a huge communal instrument (page 1298) and still retain their distinctive character.

When claves are made as a communal instrument, four musicians can play simultaneously. In a situation like this, wide variations in technique can be anticipated.

Claves: Rhythm Sticks

In Latin American dance orchestras, the rhythm is accentuated by the continual tapping of the claves (pronounced *klah-veys*), rounded sticks of solid wood 6 to 8 inches long. They are played by balancing one stick on the fingertips of one hand and tapping it lightly with the other (photograph opposite). If you hold the lower clave tightly and whack away, you will get nothing but a dull thunk.

In my version of the claves for festival use—made of 1-inch dowels—four people can play simultaneously. With plastic coated wire (see Craftnotes, page 1293), I have hung several sets from a small wooden table. (You could also make claves of straight, dry hardwood branches with the bark stripped off.) Claves can be hung in many ways, but I find that people enjoy facing each other when they play. That way they can hear one another's rhythms better.

By drawing nails in a wooden block across the serrations in a guiro, this young man will discover a scratchy new rhythmic sound.

Many hands sawing make quick work of creating a 6-foot-long guiro or scratcher. Helpers brace the length of plastic pipe as teen-agers create a serrated side by making shallow cuts along the pipe.

If It's a Guiro, Scratch It!

This plastic guiro, also known as a scratcher, or reso-reso, is the modern counterpart of a serrated gourd. It is played by scratching across the top of the serrations. Once again, PVC pipe (see plastic drums, page 1289) is the basis for the instrument, which can be any length. Teen-agers like to make guiros, using ordinary cross-cut hand saws. To serrate the pipe, set it on two sawhorses and wedge each end between large nails or blocks of wood nailed to the sawhorses to cradle the pipe and keep it from rolling (photograph above). Make cuts about ½ inch apart and very shallow—not more than ½ inch deep.

The guiro scratcher is a small rectangular block of wood with three finishing nails driven into one end. Drill a hole through the block, and join it to the pipe just as the beaters are joined to the drum (Figure A, page 1289). A guiro 6 feet long, like the one pictured, should have four or five scratchers attached along its length, more, if you like. Alternatively, short lengths of guiro can be attached to pipe mounts (like drums—page 1293), but they should be bolted on horizontally.

Brilliantly painted gongs made of fiber-barrel lids are classified as visual instruments—those that are likely to be better to see than to hear.

Graphic Arts
The visual instruments

Interesting to look at, but not too resonant or exciting to hear, are the gongs and chimes pictured on this page and page 1287. As visual instruments, their primary function is to brighten up the scene and give it a festive note. They also give instrument makers a chance to display their graphic skills. The round flat gongs are made from the tin lids of fiber barrels; when suspended and struck with foam-padded drum sticks, they produce a light, ceremonious tone. They can also be mounted on a pipe mount and played with metal or wooden beaters (below).

A much weightier gong can be made from a worn-out automobile brake drum; it is also visually interesting and will last forever. In the photograph on page 1287, you can see that this object has a shape which seems perfectly suited to its new function as a percussion instrument. You should not have to pay for brake drums; they are often discarded at auto shops and gas stations. You will probably need to give them a good cleaning, however, using a wire brush and a rust solvent. When the drum is clean, have a heavy spike bent into a u-shape and welded to the top at a welding shop (Figure C) to form a handle. You will hang the drum from this loop; so be sure the weld is built up on both ends of the loop, for maximum strength.

After the brake drum has been welded, clean off any residue and give it a thin coat of metal-primer paint. This gives you a fresh base on which to apply your designs. Water-based or acrylic paints are easy to clean up and safe for children to use. For ways of hanging heavy instruments such as brake drums and coil springs, see Craftnotes, opposite.

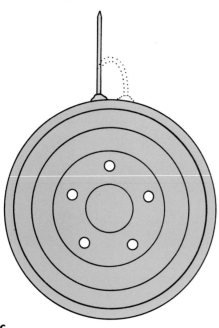

C
Figure C: A heavy spike welded to an automobile brake drum and bent into a loop makes a safe handle for this metal gong.

Coil-Spring Chimes
Automobile coil springs can be salvaged the same way as brake drums, then cleaned, painted and hung with padlocked chains. Be certain the chains are attached so they cannot slip off the coil; someone might get hurt if they did. Brightly painted coils hanging with barrel lid gongs have a festive look, especially when they are spinning between crepe paper streamers.

Automobile coil-spring gongs, painted bright colors and hung from pipe scaffolding, add color and interest to the festival scene.

A fiber-barrel lid can also be bolted to the top of a pipe mount and played like a cymbal with wood or metal beaters hung from below.

Metal Beaters
A metal beater is best for making a loud sound with a gong or chime. An excellent beater can be made by welding several nuts screwed to the tip of a long bolt (see number 8, page 1287). Such beaters—chains, too—can be colored by dipping them into thin paint and hanging them to drip-dry.

CRAFTNOTES: STANDS AND MOUNTS FOR FESTIVAL INSTRUMENTS

The stands and mounts for festival in-struments are made from plumbing pipe, pipe unions (below) and two types of interchangeable bases: a lightweight metal tripod that can be salvaged from an old music stand (see page 1289) or purchased and 2-gallon or 5-gallon concrete-filled pails (described below) suitable for heavy use outdoors. Instru-ments mounted on a pipe stem can easily be switched from one type of base to the other by the use of a pipe union.

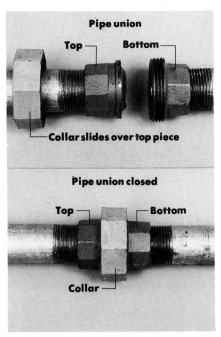

The Pipe Union

The photographs above show how a three-part pipe union is used to join two lengths of pipe. All bases are fitted with the bottom-threaded piece; all pipe stems are fitted with the top-threaded piece and the collar that goes with it. The collar slides over part of the top piece and screws onto the bottom piece, hold-ing the two pipes together. The pipe union seems to be an exception to the rule that American pipe fittings have stand-ardized threads. The important inner threads of the union differ from one brand to another; so buy them all of the same brand and the size to fit the pipe you select. The bases illustrated use ¾-inch pipe. If you fit all bases (tripods as well as concrete-filled pails) with the bottom part of the pipe union and all pipe-stem mounts with the top piece and collar, you can switch bases around to accommodate your needs.

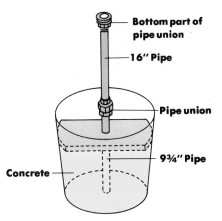

Concrete-Filled Pail Base

The drawing above shows a 2-gallon pail fitted with a block of wood shaped to fit the contour of the pail and drilled to receive a 9¾-inch length of ¾-inch pipe. When the bottom part of a pipe union is screwed onto the upper end of the pipe it should clear the top of the pail but stop short of the handle in carrying position. This lets you carry the base without scraping your knuckles on the pipe. The bottom end of the pipe in the pail should be flattened with a hammer, so it will be more firmly embedded in the concrete. Pour concrete into the pail inserting the wood block when the pail is about ¾ full. Then add more concrete until it reaches just below the threads of the pipe union. This allows room for a pipe wrench if you ever need to change union parts. When the concrete has hard-ened, the base is finished, but it should be painted for eye-appeal. Any instrument mount that has the upper half of the pipe union and collar can be fastened it.

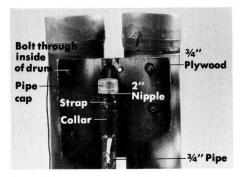

Drum Mount

The photograph above shows a way to mount drums on a pipe stem. The drum shells have been drilled and bolted to a plywood face from the inside; the plywood is held on the pipe stem with a strap and collar. A small guiro can be mounted hori-zontally with the same system.

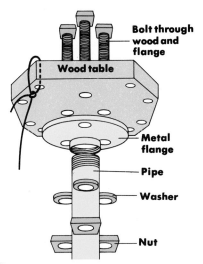

Claves Mount

The drawing above—an exploded view—shows how a small wooden table-top can be attached to a pipe mount with a metal flange and bolts; the four sets of claves are then at-tached with knotted cords to the table (see page 1290).

Hanging Instruments

The heaviest instruments—the gongs made from brake drums and coil springs—must be hung so there is no chance they will fall. Use heavy chains latched with padlocks to hang them from a support strong enough so it will not collapse and stable enough so it will not tip over. The best support we have found is a cross-braced 4-by-6-foot unit of lightweight scaf-folding, which can be rented from a scaffolding company. It is easy to transport. As an alternative, you might make use of the kind of gym-nastic climbing bar found in parks.

The barrel-lid gongs are light enough to hang almost anywhere, even from tree branches. Drums that are not pipe-mounted can be lashed anywhere in clusters so they can be played easily.

If you find a place to support a 5-foot marimba or a 6-foot guiro, for example, put a gong or a drum nearby. The guiro is very light and can be lashed anywhere with rope, but a marimba built on 2-by-4 risers is heavy and needs the support of a pair of wooden sawhorses. You can hang plastic shakers with braided ropes from any convenient support, along with streamers, banners and signs.

A student in an instrument-making workshop at the college level tests the tone of wood marimba bars cut to varying lengths.

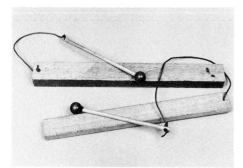

The marimba in its simplest form—the lap marimba— is a bar of wood selected for its pleasing tone, then drilled at one end to receive a cord with a wood-tipped beater attached.

Performing Arts
Marimba of many forms $ 👫 ✈ 🔨

In a marimba, as in a xylophone, a set of tuned bars is suspended or supported in such a way that each one can vibrate freely when struck, but they are held together when the instrument is moved about. The origin of the marimba is obscure. It probably appeared first in Africa before traveling to Java and Central America. It now takes many forms throughout the world, and the materials that make its music vary with the locale. Marimbas have been made of wood (including bamboo), bone, and metals in bar or tubular form. When amplified electronically, the marimba becomes a vibraphone (occasionally called a vibraharp).

When you build a marimba with wooden bars, as suggested here, a basic law regulating pitch becomes apparent: length affects it. Other factors being equal, a longer bar will have a lower pitch than a shorter bar. But both bars must have exactly the same characteristics—kind of wood, moisture content, cross-section dimensions—for this to be true.

Wood Sounds Good
Any piece of wood may have an excellent tone. Let your ear be the final judge. But when you choose wood, discard any piece with worm holes, a crack, or a large knot or knothole within the sounding area, or a piece which for any reason does not match the other pieces being included. There can be a great variation in both tone and pitch between two different pieces of wood from the same tree; yet pieces of wood from totally different sources may sound very much alike.

Bob Wood and friends demonstrate one way of playing the lap marimba. Additional bars without beaters can be added to your knees until your lap is full.

Musical Knees: the Lap Marimba

The easiest introduction to marimba-making is the lap marimba (opposite) which starts with a bar of wood with a beater attached at one end. You rest this on your knees with about a quarter of its length projecting on each side. The two points touching the knees are called nodes, which are points of reduced vibration. The beater is usually made from a 1/4- to 5/16-inch dowel with a round wooden bead glued on the end. If you buy the beads first, you can choose dowels to fit them. Before attaching the beaters, lay at least two pieces of wood across your knees and tap on them to test their tone and pitch. If you don't like the sound, try other bars. After you have selected two bars, attach a beater to each with 24-inch lengths of insulated wire or twine (opposite). This will enable you to play with both hands. You can add as many other marimba bars as your lap will hold, but only two need to have beaters attached unless you want to try two in each hand.

A marimba à l'Africaine strung between two poles looks improvised but sounds just as good as the more permanent versions on the following pages.

Marimba bars, strung à l'Africaine and hung over this girl's shoulders, transform her into a walking musical instrument which can be played with a little help from her friends.

Marimba à l'Africaine

Stringing bars together with cord makes the instrument more permanent and portable, and you can tune it to a scale (see page 1296). The bars can also be arranged at random as long as you find their tones pleasing. For the cord, drill a hole through the end of each bar. String both sides simultaneously, and make large knots between bars. You can determine drilling points by resting the bar on a pair of soft supporting ropes, each about 1/5 the length of the bar from each end. Play the bar; then move the rope in 1/4-inch at a time and test the sound. Mark the wood where the tone sounds best and drill at that point. A rope marimba can be strung between two trees, hung around your neck or waist, or draped over the shoulders while it is being played.

What could be funkier than a marimba skirt that sounds like a wind chime when you walk?

1295

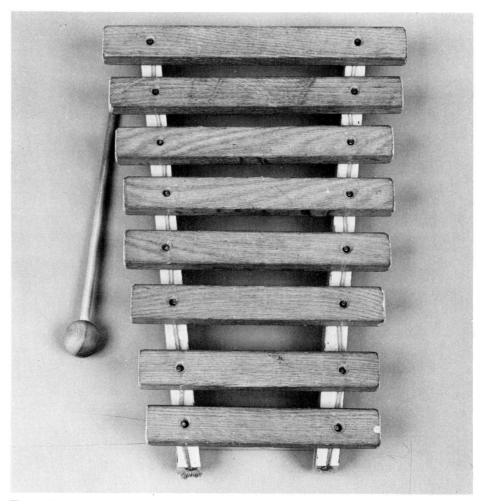

The wooden bars of this one-octave marimba have been tuned to play a scale. The bars rest on cords stapled to the risers which allow the bars to vibrate freely when they are struck with a wooden beater.

A Tuned, One-Octave Marimba

In cultures where music is written out so it can be duplicated by others, marimbas are often tuned to established scales. But our festival marimbas are deliberately non-melodic, so participants do not feel compelled to produce tunes. Scales can be used, of course. Three- or five-note scales don't pose the difficulties that an eight-note scale presents; yet you can develop catchy, interesting melodic bits on them. But if you would like to make an eight-note-tuned marimba, this is how to do it: get about 11 feet of wood with identical cross-section dimensions. You might try pieces of 1/2-by-2-inch wood, sometimes called furring strips. Look for pieces without knotholes or other imperfections. The measurements given here are meant only to clarify the idea. Variations such as graining and moisture content affect the tone and pitch as much as length and width; so you will have to use your ear as the final judge, not the yardstick.

Start with the lowest pitch possible—that is, the longest piece that will give you a pleasant tone. Try a piece 12 to 14 inches long and about 1/2 inch thick as your bottom note; shorten it if necessary to get a good tone. Now cut a piece 3 to 5 inches shorter than this first piece and test its tone. You want it to be close to being one octave above the first tone bar. These two pieces are your top and bottom notes. Measure the length of both bars, find the difference in length and divide it by seven. This will give you the average length to increase each tone bar starting from the shortest. For example, if your lowest tone bar is 13 1/2 inches long and your highest is 10 inches long, the difference—3 1/2—divided by 7 gives you 1/2 inch. So the bars would increase in length by 1/2 inch from 10 up. When you have cut these bars, they will still be tuned only approximately.

Fine Tuning

The bars must now be fine-tuned individually. You can raise the pitch by shortening a bar a little at a time, or lower the pitch by filing a notch under the middle of the bar (Figure D) with a coarse file (or by cutting another bar a bit longer). You may need a piano to help you judge the pitch as you tune the bars. After the bars have been satisfactorily tuned, they can be drilled and attached to the supporting risers (Figure E). Drilling will not affect the pitch noticeably.

Framing

The picture opposite shows a framed marimba with a base that tapers to accommodate the diminishing length of the bars. The risers that support the bars can be nailed to a flat surface, or they can be part of a frame closed at both ends. The bars lie across the risers but do not rest directly on them. A piece of insulated wire or cord stapled to the surface of the frame (Figure E), acts as a cushion between the bars and the risers, letting the bars vibrate when struck. But don't staple this cushioning cord in place until you have determined the position of each bar on the riser and have drilled the first hole. The cords wind around the drilled holes and are stapled to the risers in spaces between the bars. This keeps the bar from rattling against the metal staple.

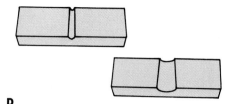

D

Figure D: To lower the pitch of a bar, notch it on the bottom side with a rat-tail file or saw.

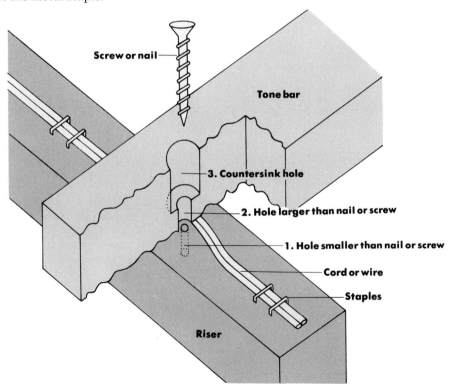

Screw or nail

Tone bar

3. Countersink hole

2. Hole larger than nail or screw

1. Hole smaller than nail or screw

Cord or wire

Staples

Riser

E

Figure E: To attach the marimba bars to the risers so they are free to vibrate, drill three holes at each joint, the smallest (1) through bar and into the riser, one larger than the screw or nail (2) through the bar only, and one large enough (3) to countersink the head of the screw or nail beneath the surface so the beater will not hit it. Plastic-covered electrical cord, held with staples between bars, permits vibrations.

Drilling

Holding a bar across the risers in position, begin with a drill bit smaller than the nail or screw you will be using. Drill through the tone bar and into the riser; this is the receiving hole. When you have drilled a hole on each end of the bar, lift the bar off the riser and use a drill bit slightly larger than your nail or screw to enlarge the first hole through the bar. A third drilling makes a countersink hole a bit larger than the head of the nail or screw and about 1/4 inch deep. When drilling a countersink hole, hold the bar firmly and do not let it climb up the drill bit or it might go completely through. If this happens, the bar is spoiled. It is necessary to countersink the nails or screws so the beaters do not hit them and wear out quickly.

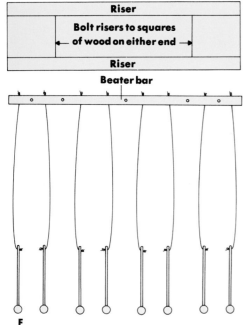

F

Figure F: A top view of the frame for the marimba pictured at right is shown above. Risers are bolted at the ends to squares of 1-inch lumber; this assembly is supported by sawhorses. Long strips of wood bolted to the sides of the risers provide an efficient way of attaching many beaters at one time.

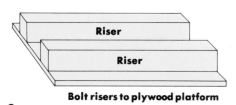

G

Figure G: A marimba can also be framed by first cutting a solid base from one piece of 3/4-inch plywood, then attaching risers directly to it. Beaters can then be attached to the plywood base.

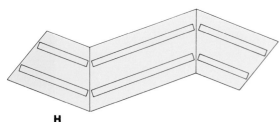

H

Figure H: When a plywood base is cut with angled ends, marimbas can be constructed to form modules of interesting shapes when placed end to end. (A circular marimba is pictured opposite.)

A large mother marimba, with 2-by-6 risers, has bars arranged in 4-tone groupings.

The Mother Marimba

The mother marimba, originally 20 feet long and built for a festival in New York's Central Park, was too large to transport or store easily. After the festival I cut the frame into 5-foot lengths, adding braces on the ends. For subsequent festivals, these parts were lined up on sawhorses. Since then I have had a recurring dream of a whole string of marimbas, each about 4 feet long, stretching in a winding line through a meadow and over a hill, disappearing in the distance, each being played by about fifteen people.

This large communal marimba is the heart of the festival orchestra. It can be built in several ways. Figure F and the photograph above show one type built on a parallel frame, with risers made from 2 by 6's joined and braced with squares of 1-inch lumber at either end. Another method is to attach the risers to a base cut from one piece of plywood (Figure G).

Marimbas with gracefully curved contours can be made by cutting free-form shapes for bases from sheets of plywood, using a sabre saw, band saw or large jigsaw. However, cutting risers for these shapes requires a lot of measuring. You can get a similar effect much easier by cutting rectangular bases with angled ends (Figure H). This gives you a modular system that allows you to assemble various shapes with the marimba sections. To avoid the problem of placing tone bars across angled ends, leave them off where the angle begins.

Tune and Tone

Although I don't believe that a festival marimba should be tuned to a conventional scale, I sometimes build marimbas with repeated 3-note or 5-note patterns. The bars are not tuned exactly but are close in tonal range. However, a marimba made entirely of bars of random tones is satisfying to hear and play. A 5-foot-long marimba whose tones range from high to low pitch would resemble the small tuned marimba on page 1296.

There is a limit to the rule that a larger bar gives a lower pitch. You cannot continue increasing the length of a piece of wood indefinitely and expect the tone to get increasingly deeper; at some point you must also increase the cross-section dimensions. For example, if you start by cutting bars with a cross-section of 1/2 by 2 inches, at some point the tone will be lost. Then you have to switch to a larger cross-section, perhaps 1 by 3 or even 2 by 4.

Remember to make the frame fit the bars *after* you have tested and chosen them for the instrument. If you plan to build several instruments, it helps enormously to have the use of a power saw and a drill press. When cutting the base, allow a large enough lip so you will have a place to attach the beaters.

Resonators

Most professionally-built marimbas (or xylophones) have resonators under each tone bar. These are small sounding-boxes that increase volume. You may be able to demonstrate the effect of a resonator by putting a lap marimba across your knees and holding a can, open at one end, under it as you tap the bar. The resonance of the air in the can must match the resonance of the tone bar. As you bring the can close to the bar (if indeed you have found the right-sized can for your piece of wood), tone and volume will increase noticeably. This is an area of research entirely open for your experiments. The superstructure needed to support resonator containers would make the instrument more bulky and fragile, but the improvement of tone would be impressive.

Crowdsmanship

Suppose you make all of these instruments and nobody wants to play them—have courage. This may happen occasionally during any festival as people move around. There will also be times when everyone wants to play at once—sometimes for a half-hour without changing the beat.

If I sense that a group needs encouragement, I might play along on a conga drum to help get things started. Sometimes the group may enjoy playing along with a short segment of music recorded on tape.

Left to their own devices, people do fascinating things with rhythms. At one festival, I taped a session that was truly remarkable, then played it back to the astonished group that had just performed it. People are continually surprising themselves—and others—with their spontaneous music-making abilities.

For related entries, see "Dulcimers," "Whistles and Flutes," "Parades and Festivals," "Stagecraft."

Strangers share a moment of rhythm-making.

A marimba produces the kind of music that makes you smile, even if you have never had the good fortune of playing before.

Students at Fairleigh Dickinson College in New Jersey enjoy playing on a circular walk-in marimba.

All bundled up for a winter festival, this group finds that a good beat keeps them warm.

1299

NAPKIN FOLDING
A Feast for the Eyes

Poppy Cannon, formerly food editor of Ladies Home Journal, Town and Country, House Beautiful *and* Mademoiselle, *served as a consultant for this article. Author of many cookbooks, Poppy was one of three American women honored in France with the title of* Commandeur *of the* Chevaliers du Tastevin, *the Society of Burgundian Winetasters, was inducted into the* Commanderie des Bordeaux *which is traditionally closed to women, and was made a* Commandeur de la Commanderie des Cordon Bleu *for her contributions to gastronomy.*

Descriptions of elaborate dinner parties given in the seventeenth, eighteenth and even into the nineteenth century remark on the importance of napkin folding as an essential decoration for tables set in the grand manner. Today, except among caterers, little attention is paid to this simple but lovely art. You can have a great deal of fun and delight your guests by reviving it for special occasions.

It was long thought that stylized folding could be done only with dinner napkins made of double damask—a firm, lustrous double-woven fabric. Isabella Mary Beeton, author of *Mrs. Beeton's Hints to Housewives*, published in 1868, recommended 18 such table napkins, each 30 inches square, for a household of four. She said it was absolutely useless to attempt anything but the most simple folded forms unless the napkins were slightly starched and smoothly ironed. For ordinary family use at that time, napkins were usually folded simply and slipped through napkin rings; each family member had a fresh napkin for each day, and it was reused at each meal. Most elaborate napkin folding was used to ornament the table for special occasions. Mrs. Beeton warned that when an intricately folded design was chosen, the folding had to be precise or the result would look slovenly.

Exactness and intricacy were goals sought by the folders of the starched napkins of Mrs. Beeton's day, but experiments will show you that simple, elegant designs with only a few folds can be created with drip-dry fabric napkins and even with paper napkins. As a matter of fact, napkin folding parallels the Japanese paper-folding art of origami, since some of the same basic shapes are used in both.

The Ritz Hotel in London and to a lesser extent the Ritz in Madrid are among the few places left where a tradition of napkin folding still exists, and even there, it is reserved for special occasions. Curiously, at the Ritz in London, napkins are given elaborate folds for room service. Society caterers still use specially folded napkins for an elegant touch at weddings and other ceremonious occasions.

Although August Escoffier, the chef so closely associated with César Ritz, seems to have left no written instructions on the subject of napkin folding, both he and Ritz paid a great deal of attention to this aspect of table decoration in the latter part of the nineteenth century. Ritz and Escoffier were innovators and simplifiers at the same time. On at least one occasion, César Ritz spoke scornfully of the fact that 26 shapes of napkin folding had been popular in the seventeenth century. Many of these had fallen into disuse in his day, but it was his opinion that too many still survived. He felt it was about time to forget such folds as Noah's ark, hen and chickens, tortoises and rabbits. But he favored retaining fans, palm leaves, candles, boats, and roses (the latter sometimes called artichokes). All of these are still appropriate on a contemporary dinner table and are not difficult to make. To duplicate the folded shapes on the pages that follow, you can use either drip-dry napkins or 3-ply paper napkins at least 16 inches square. Or, if you have them, starched and folded double damask napkins are still impressive. Before you fold cloth napkins, iron them flat so there will be no creases in the finished shape.

Cloth napkins folded in a palm-leaf shape are simple to make, yet they are an elegant addition to this pretty table setting. The solid blue color contrasts nicely with the patterned plates.

Figure A

Paper Folding and Cutting
The palm leaf

The palm leaf, pictured in color on page 1301, will look fuller if it is made with a cloth napkin, but a paper napkin can be used. To make the palm leaf, follow the steps illustrated in Figure A (left). Fold the napkin into quarters (step 1). Then fold in half diagonally (step 2). Place this fold on the bottom and pleat the triangle (step 3). Do not press the pleats into the fabric; this shape is based on soft, rounded folds. Keep the flat edge on the bottom as you put the napkin in a glass; the folds that are above the rim of the glass will open slightly so the napkin resembles a palm leaf.

A bright red-and-white napkin boat sailing on an ocean of dark blue makes an enticing table setting for a child. It is simple enough for the child to fold himself.

Paper Folding and Cutting
The sailboat

The sailboat fold is easy enough for a child to make and provides a whimsical addition to a table set for children. To form the sailboat, follow the steps illustrated in Figure B; fold the napkin in half to form a triangle (step 1). With this diagonal fold as the base of the triangle, fold the sides into the center (step 2). Fold up the points that are below the base of the triangle (step 3). Then fold the base of the triangle up so it covers the lower point (step 4), thus forming the hull of the boat.

Figure B

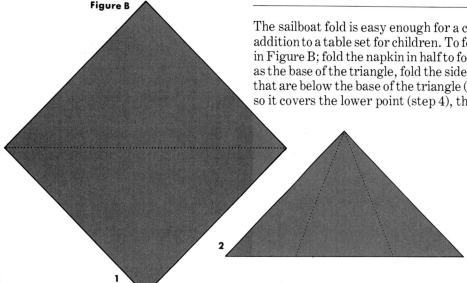

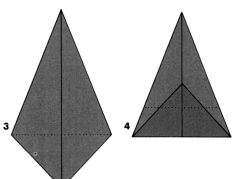

Paper Folding and Cutting
The candle

The candle napkin will stand by itself even when it is made with a paper napkin. To make a candle, follow the steps in Figure C. Fold the napkin into a triangle (step 1). Fold up the bottom edge to form a cuff about 1½ inches wide (step 2). Roll the napkin tightly with the cuff on the outside (step 3). Tuck the end corner into the cuff to hold the rolled shape in place and turn down the upper point of the triangle so it resembles a flickering flame.

Figure C

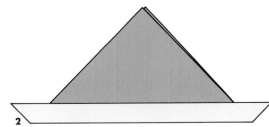

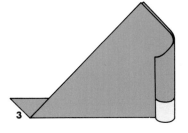

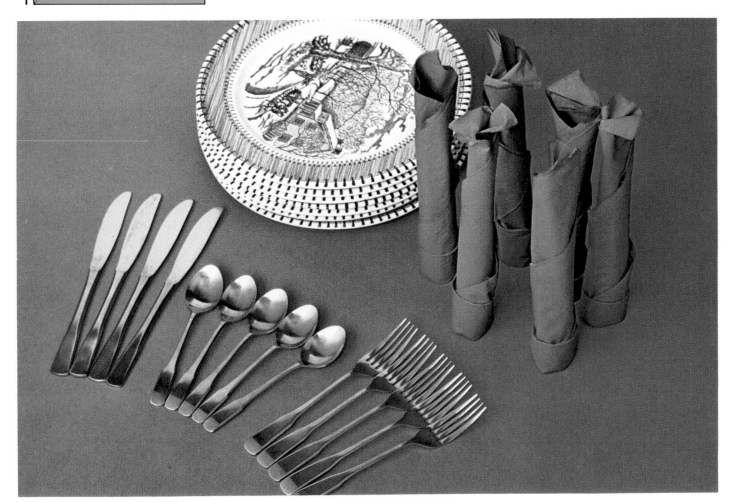

The fold that gives you these upright candles provides an easy way for guests to pick up napkins from a heavily-laden buffet table. They also take up less space on the table.

An attractive and simple way to set a table for lunch or a light snack is to slip the silverware in the napkin pocket.

A green paper napkin folded into a lily shape echoes the pattern on the plate to make an appealing table setting.

Figure D

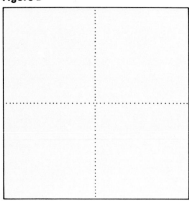

1

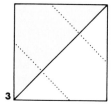

2

3

Paper Folding and Cutting
The pocket

The pocket is a quick way to fold a napkin so it will hold silverware. To make the pocket, follow the steps in Figure D. Fold the napkin in quarters (step 1). Turn the napkin so the folded corner (the corner that was the center of the napkin) is on the bottom right and the corner that is made up of four layers is on the top left. Fold down one point, the top layer, so that it meets the bottom corner (step 2), thus forming a pocket. Fold the sides under (step 3). Place the napkin in the center of the plate and put silverware in the pocket.

Paper Folding and Cutting
The lily

A paper napkin makes an attractive lily because the layers of paper can be separated to form the petals. To make the lily, follow the steps illustrated in Figure E. Fold the napkin in half to form a triangle (step 1). Pleat this triangle as shown (step 2). Place the base of the triangle in a glass with folds pressing against the sides of the glass. Separate the two points of the triangle to balance the napkin; then peel apart the layers of the napkin to make light, airy petals.

Figure E

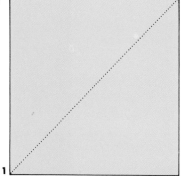

1

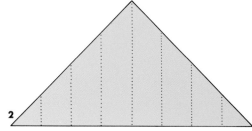

2

Paper Folding and Cutting
The band

¢ 🗙 👫 🍲

To make this elegant napkin shape, follow the steps in Figure F. Fold the napkin in quarters (step 1). Fold back the upper corner of the top layer so it meets the opposite bottom corner (step 2). Fold this point back up toward its original position, thus making a diagonal band about 1 inch wide (step 3). Tuck in the point that extends past the center diagonal fold (step 4). Bring the upper corner of the next layer of the napkin to the center fold (step 5). Bring the fold made in step 5 to the center fold (step 6), thus forming another diagonal band about 1 inch wide. Fold the diagonally opposite corners under (step 7). Place the napkin in the center of the plate or to the left of the forks.

Figure F

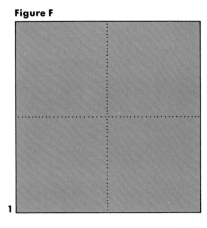

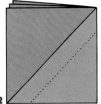
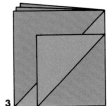
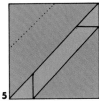
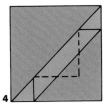
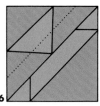
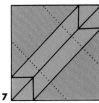

A napkin folded to form a band adds straight lines that are a good foil for the rounded lines of the patterned silverware, china and glassware.

Figure G

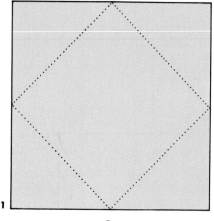

A bright blue artichoke sitting on a daintily-patterned plate adds an amusing touch to a formal table setting. An intricate-looking folded shape, the artichoke is actually quite simple.

Paper Folding and Cutting
The artichoke

The artichoke, also called a rose or a water lily, is an intricately folded shape that goes well with a formal place setting. To make the artichoke, follow the folds illustrated in Figure G. Fold the corners of the napkin into the center (step 1). Repeat this with the newly-formed corners (step 2), and the napkin will look like the one in step 3. Turn the napkin over (step 4) and turn the corners into the center once again (step 5). Hold the napkin down firmly in the center with a glass so the points that are in the center do not move, and pull out each of the corners from underneath (step 6). Carefully place the napkin in the center of a plate.

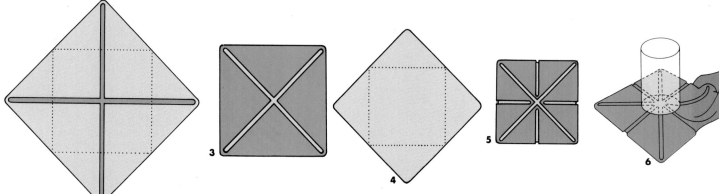

Figure H

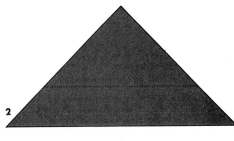

A fleur-de-lis stands proudly at attention because it is made from a cloth napkin and its base is anchored in a napkin ring.

Paper Folding and Cutting
The fleur-de-lis

Although the fleur-de-lis looks complicated, it is a surprisingly easy shape to make—as shown in the illustrations in Figure H. First, fold the napkin in half diagonally (step 1) forming a triangle. Then fold the base of the triangle upward, about one-third the total height (step 2). Pleat this shape (step 3). Place the flat edge of the napkin in a napkin ring and pull out the leaves on either side. The fleur-de-lis can be placed in the center of the plate or on the table above the plate.

Paper Folding and Cutting
The fan

The fan is the simplest of all napkin shapes to fold, but it can be given a look of sophistication by folding two paper napkins of harmonious colors together. Following Figure I, fold each napkin in half to form a rectangle (step 1). Place one color on top of the other, exposing about two inches of the bottom napkin (step 2). Pleat these two napkins together as if they were one (step 3). Place the bottom of the napkin in a glass with folds facing the plate and fan out the pleats.

Figure I

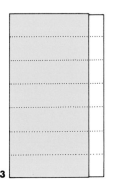

When making the fan, choose two colors that harmonize with your table setting.

NECKTIES
Fit to Be Tied

Jane Mensch-Mutshnick is a freelance illustrator who paints ties (seashells, too) as a hobby. She began designing ties by making one for her husband. After his co-workers and friends saw it, Jane was swamped with orders for personalized ties. A graduate of the Tyler School of Art in Philadelphia, Jane has worked as an art director and a children's book illustrator. Her work has been shown at New York galleries.

Men have used collars, scarves, ruffles, lace and ribbons as neck decorations for many centuries, but the cravat, the forerunner of today's necktie, is a relatively modern invention. It dates from the seventeenth century and the reign of Louis XIV of France. Troops from the German province of Croatia, employed by King Louis for his palace guard, are credited with the custom of tying a folded strip of fabric around the neck. Impressed by their dashing neckpieces, Louis himself adopted the look and it quickly caught on in Paris and across the continent. Later centuries saw the cravat shortened and fastened tightly around the neck, or loosely folded and knotted or tied in a bow. The four-in-hand tie, presently popular, dates from the last half of the nineteenth century.

While neckties evolved according to how they were worn, interest in ties now centers on design. The neckties pictured in this entry are individual; each was designed to fit the taste of its owner. The technique of drawing on fabric with colorfast markers is easy to learn but it takes practice to perfect.

As an alternate neckpiece, you can create a colorful scarf from a man's handkerchief and paint a design with fabric paint. And, if you are burdened with a rackful of old neckties, a suggestion for recycling them into a wearable garment is on page 1316. All the projects in this entry are inexpensive and require few materials.

Create a Conversation Piece

A custom-made illustrated tie adds a one-of-a-kind neckpiece to your wardrobe. It also makes an unusual gift for a friend. Most ties can be finished in just a few hours. The designs are drawn on solid-color ties with permanent-ink felt-tip markers. The designs are then colored in, also with markers. You have a lot of leeway in creating and coloring designs. The technique is quite simple, much like working on a child's coloring-book illustration. The markers look different on fabric than on paper, however; techniques for experimenting with them are on page 1310.

As to the nature of the illustrations, the possibilities are unlimited. Draw anything that suits your fancy. A tie that reflects the personality of its future owner is fun to draw, and such ties are instant conversation pieces. But keep the design simple, at least for the first few ties you attempt. The doodle tie on page 1312 combines abstract shapes with the owner's astrological sign and initials. Even with such an uncomplicated pattern, it is hard to predict exactly what will happen when you color in the outlined design. You might decide to alter the color scheme as you work, or the markers might bleed slightly, giving the design a free-flowing look. You should feel free to make changes, if necessary, as you work.

Most ties are designed for men, but there is no reason why any of these ties could not be worn by a woman. Many women, of course, favor scarves, and you can use the same techniques to make a colorful and feminine neckerchief or work with fabric paint, as described on page 1315.

Louis XIV popularized the cravat in the seventeenth century, and even employed an official *cravatier* to arrange the official ends.

Artist Jane Mensch-Mutshnick and her husband Irv wear their fantasies up front on his illustrated necktie and her hand-painted scarf while mixing at an informal cocktail party. Directions for the tie start on page 1311; see page 1315 for the scarf.

1: Colorfast felt-tipped markers with points of various sizes are the principal tools used for decorating neckties with custom designs.

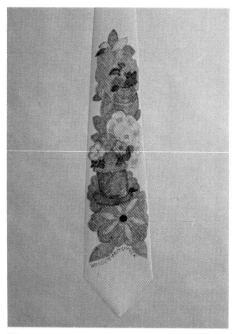

The weave of the fabric influences the outcome of the design. Here, a textured green polyester fabric adds interest to a simple floral illustration.

Tools and Materials

To begin, you need a tie. It can be purchased or made from scratch, using the pattern and instructions on page 1314. The tie should be white or a fairly light color; markers do not show up well on dark fabrics. The tie's width, shape and fabric depend on your preferences. Those pictured here range from 4 to 5 inches in width at the bottom and are 52 inches long, but any size can be used. When choosing a fabric or buying a ready-made tie, look for medium-weight cotton, rayon, cotton blends and polyesters. Avoid silk; it is difficult to work with because it is slippery and because colors bleed more on silk than on other fabrics. A tie with a definite weave, such as the flowered green tie below, left, is a challenge to decorate because the design must take the weave into account. If you plan a busy, bold design, work on a smooth fabric.

The easiest tie to color is one with a white background because it is easiest to imagine what colors will look like on white. If you work on a colored fabric, take into account that colors change their appearance. Yellow applied on a green background, for example, looks yellow-green rather than pure yellow.

In addition to the tie, you will need an assortment of felt-tipped markers. These may be purchased individually or in sets. They come in a wide range of colors and point sizes. Those most useful have interchangeable nibs (felt tips). Thin nibs are necessary for lettering and outlining, and broad points are best for coloring in outlined areas.

The markers should contain a permanent, waterproof ink so the colors won't fade or run if the tie gets wet. Unfortunately, not all permanent markers are equally permanent, so you should test each marker on a scrap of fabric before using it. Draw several lines with the marker to see whether the color runs. If it does, try a different brand. To see how much the marker will bleed on the actual tie, draw a small line or two on the back where it won't show. All colors will run at least a little, and some bleed more than others. You can learn how each will work only by trying it on a fabric.

To be certain the colors will be permanent, use textile paints instead of felt-tipped markers. These are recommended for the neckerchief on page 1315. Textile paints, however, are somewhat more difficult to apply than marker inks; they are quite messy, and they must be used in a room with good ventilation. Since a hand-painted necktie is rarely cleaned, markers are recommended for ties.

The only other material you need is a can of spray-on moisture repellent. This fabric protector makes the completed tie stain-resistant.

Planning a Tie Design

First decide what kind of design you want to make. An illustrated tie has a picture on it and may tell a story or just repeat a realistic motif like a flower or a horse. An abstract design is just that—a non-realistic composition such as the one on the opposite page. Both kinds of ties may be personalized by incorporating the wearer's initials or symbols representing his hobbies, profession or appearance.

A number of design ideas are on page 1313. They can be used full size on a tie or scarf, but are meant only as suggestions. Once you know what you want to draw, work out your own design on a piece of paper the size of the tie. This will make it easier to position the design on the tie later on.

After outlining the design on paper, color it with markers to make sure you like the effect. It is better to experiment on paper at this stage than when working on the tie itself, especially if you are working with markers on fabric for the first time.

Using Drawing Markers

Practicing with markers will show you how fine or thick a line you can draw and how the colors look together. Markers can also be used like water colors with one color applied over another to achieve a third. When you do this, start with light shades and then apply darker shades for interesting blends.

When you paint the tie, remember that unplanned occurrences often result in more exciting designs. If you were drawing the thin-lined tree tie (page 1309) and the marker line came out heavier than you had planned, the effect might please you more than the original, even though it would appear less delicately drawn.

As this light brown tie illustrates, markers can be used on a colored background effectively. The abstract design was strictly a product of the artist's imagination, and she modified the design as the illustration progressed.

Paint and Color
Tree tie design

The step-by-step procedures for making the tree tie design (shown in the photographs on the next page), apply to making any of the designs in this entry and to illustrating ties in general. As you will see, much depends on the type of fabric you are working with and how the markers affect the fabric.

Pastel colors were selected for the tree tie (pictured on page 1309), to give a soft, muted effect. The design was planned so that the top butterfly would be on the knot. To use the tree design on page 1313, copy it on a sheet of tracing paper, modifying it if you like. Then move the paper around on the front of the tie until you find a position to your liking. It's helpful to wear the tie yourself or have someone model it as you experiment with the design, especially if you want the butterfly at the knot.

This design is simple enough to be drawn freehand on the tie. In fact, this is a better way to proceed. Even if you have had no training as an artist, with practice you will be able to make an interesting pattern.

Draw the outline of your design on the tie with a thin-pointed black or brown marker. Then fill in the various shapes with various colors. Begin with the lighter colors so that if one is not satisfactory, you can go over it with a darker color. As you

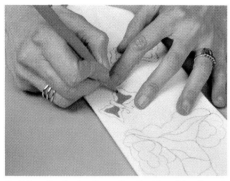

2: After the design is outlined with a thin-tipped brown marker on the tie, the centers of the butterfly wings are colored with a pink marker.

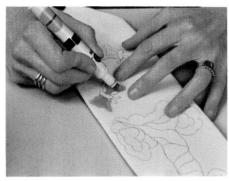

3: A broad-tipped yellow marker colors the areas around the pink sections and may overlap slightly with the pink for a softening bleed effect.

4: Fine design details like these pink dots representing butterfly wing patterns are added last to enhance the design.

5: Sections of the tree are first inked with light-colored markers; darker colors can then be applied to create a third color if desired.

6: Fine diagonal lines drawn with a thin black marker create the impression of shading details on the tree trunk.

7: The last step is to spray the completed tie with a moisture repellant to make it stain resistant and eliminate the need for cleaning.

fill in the colors, start with a rather small part of the design (in this case the butterflies). This will give you a chance to see how the markers are going to work on your particular fabric. The tie pictured is a blend of polyester and rayon, so the markers bled very little on it. The very fine design details should be saved for last. Shading used in the tree trunk is done in two steps. First, fill in an area with a broad-pointed marker. Then, using a thin-pointed marker of a darker color, go over the area with thin lines. The crosshatch effect produces a shaded look.

Once you are satisfied with the design, the tie is done. Markers dry instantly. Spray the completed tie with a moisture repellant to make it stain resistant. Place the tie on a piece of newspaper and coat it evenly, holding the spray can 6 to 8 inches from the fabric.

The artist incorporated the astrological symbol for Aries, the ram, and the initials "J.C." into the design of this doodle tie. Professional and hobby symbols are also useful for personalizing a tie.

Paint and Color
Ideas for illustrating ties

The tie at left is called a doodle tie because the design is reminiscent of the doodles one may draw while talking on the telephone. It is also an example of the spontaneity associated with tie illustrations. The design began with an overall concept of color and design that made use of squiggly lines, circles, squares, and simple shapes. As this tie was designed for a friend, his astrological sign and initials were incorporated.

The brown tie on the previous page was started as an abstraction, meant to be bold splashes of color. Then the splashes of color were tied together with lines and shapes made with a green thin-pointed marker; this combination made the tie illustration look finished.

The green-flowered tie shown on page 1310 was done in similar fashion, but the weave of the fabric gives the finished neckpiece a textured look.

A
Figure A: These designs can be transferred full size to a tie or neckerchief. All are by Jane Mensch-Mutshnick.

CRAFTNOTES: MAKING A NECKTIE

To make a 5-inch wide necktie you will need: paper and pencil for the pattern, scissors, pins, needle and thread, dressmaker's carbon paper, a toothed tracing wheel, a sewing machine and an iron. Approximately ¾ yard of fabric is required for the tie, ½ yard of woven or non-woven interfacing and ⅜ yard of a compatible fabric for the lining.

paper ruled in 1-inch squares. Transfer all the pattern markings shown and then cut out each piece. The arrows on the tie and lining pieces indicate where to place the patterns so the fabric will be cut on the bias—at a 45-degree angle to the fabric threads. Interfacing is also best cut on the bias.

center seam of the tie. Temporarily hold the interfacing in place by basting it to the tie in the center along its whole length as the dotted line indicates.

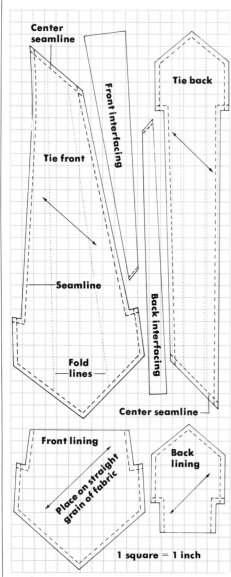

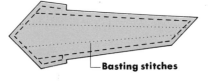

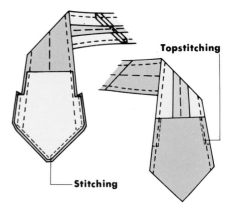

Cutting and marking
Place the tie patterns on the fabric, pin in place and cut. After cutting, use dressmaker's carbon paper and a tracing wheel to transfer all the appropriate markings. Next cut out the interfacing and lining pieces, and transfer the appropriate markings.

Sew along the fold lines on each of the main tie pieces with long basting stitches, following the dotted lines indicated. These basting stitches remain in place until the tie is finally folded to its finished size and slipstitched closed.

Attaching the lining
With right sides facing, pin the lining in place on each tie end. Stitch, following the red stitches shown in the diagram above, left. Trim seams and clip curves where necessary. Turn the lined ends rightside out and press. To further secure the lining to the tie, topstitch the lining in place following the red lines as indicated in the diagram above, right.

Finishing
Fold the right side of the tie along the fold line, and handsew it along the seamline to the interfacing, as shown above. Use a loose running stitch and make sure that stitches penetrate only the interfacing, not the front of the tie.

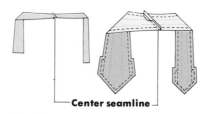

Stitching
Stitch the two interfacing pieces together at the center seam as indicated above. Trim the seam and press it open. Also stitch the center seam of the two tie pieces. Trim the seam and press it open.

Fold the left edge under along the seamline to make a ⅜-inch hem; then overlap the right edge and pin it in place along the length of the tie.

Slipstitch the seam but be careful to catch only the edge of the fabric and interfacing, not the front of the tie.

Remove all basting stitches and press the tie. Use a press cloth and press around the tie's edges rather than directly on the tie. This keeps the tie's folded edges from being too flat.

The pattern
Above are the six pattern pieces: 2 tie pieces; 2 interfacing pieces; 2 lining pieces. All pattern pieces have a ⅜-inch seam allowance all around, except the interfacing pieces which are seamed only where they join.

Enlarge the pattern pieces by copying each square of the grid shown onto

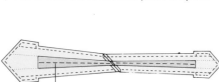

Attaching interfacing
Fit the interfacing between the basted fold lines as shown above, matching the center seam of the interfacing and the

Paint and Color
Butterfly neckerchief

¢ ⬛ ☗ ⛯

The neckerchief on page 1309 is a vibrant accessory to wear with casual sports clothes. Because textile paints were used, the scarf can be washed safely—the colors are permanent. The scarf is made of a 10-by-21-inch white cotton handkerchief but it could be any size. You might even want to make a scarf from a piece of fabric. For this neckerchief, 4-inch butterflies were painted in opposite corners. Other designs could adorn the remaining corners so a new look could be achieved simply by folding the neckerchief in a different way.

What You Need
In addition to a cotton handkerchief, you will need oil-based textile paints (sold in art supply stores). You will also need aluminum pie tins or several old plates for mixing colors and an assortment of artist's oil paint brushes—thin ones for outlining and thicker ones for filling in. Work on the floor or on a board covered with several layers of newspaper. Straight pins or push pins are used to hold the handkerchief in place while you paint. You also need an iron to set the colors once the paint has dried.

8: Like a necktie, a handkerchief scarf can be illustrated with felt-tipped markers but the colors will bleed more on a thin cotton like this than they would on a fabric woven more tightly.

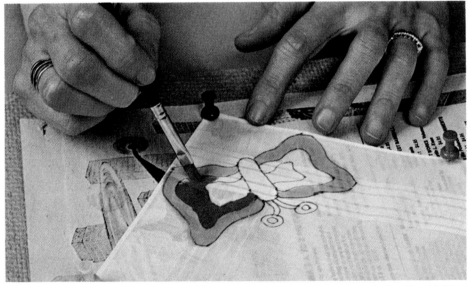

9: Cover the work surface with several thicknesses of newspaper before you pin the handkerchief in place and begin to apply fabric paint. The paper will absorb paint that penetrates the fabric.

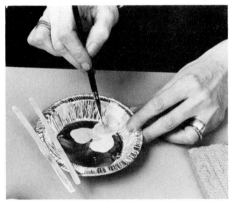

10: Use disposable aluminum pie tins to hold fabric paint and flat wooden sticks for stirrers.

Painting the Neckerchief
Wash the handkerchief in cold water to remove the sizing. After it dries, iron it and pin it to a newspaper-covered work surface, being careful to stretch it so that it is taut. The handkerchief is ready for painting. But work out the design on paper first. When you are satisfied, copy it freehand on the handkerchief with a hard pencil. Then go over the lines with a thin-tipped brown or black marker. Follow the manufacturer's directions for mixing and thinning the textile paint. If you have never used such paints, practice on scrap paper and a test piece of fabric until you can apply the paint smoothly and evenly.

As you paint the neckerchief, start with light colors. If you are not satisfied with a color after you apply it, you can go over it with a darker color. Yellow was applied first on these butterflies, then red and orange. Finally, the butterflies were outlined in black with a thin brush.

Once the design is completed, set the neckerchief aside for 24 hours to let the paint dry completely. The colors are then permanently set by pressing the painted areas lightly with a warm iron.

11: Let the paint dry for 24 hours; then press lightly with a warm iron to set the colors.

Old ties become new fashion when sewn into an ankle-length denim skirt for all seasons.

Needlecrafts
Recycled tie skirt

One novel way to make use of old neckties is to make them a part of the fabric in a long, flowing skirt. The front-opening style of the skirt in the photograph is only one possibility. Ties might be incorporated into an A-line skirt, a jumper, wide-legged pants, or any homesewn garment with simple lines. Buy a pattern for a garment and then follow the directions below for incorporating neckties into pattern sections.

The neckties are not used as is: rather, the back seam is opened, the interlining removed, and the ties pressed open to their full width. Then the tie is cut to the desired dimensions and shape (Figure B). A seam allowance of ¼ inch is allowed for sewing the tie to the skirt fabric.

First, make a paper patterns for the ties. Figure B below shows the dimensions of the pattern used to cut the ties recycled for this skirt (made for a tall woman). But it can be adapted for ties for any garment. When adjusting the pattern to your height, it is preferable to trim off extra length from the top, so you make use of the wider part of the tie that extends to the hemline.

Equipment and Materials

In addition to fabric and thread for the garment you are sewing, you need paper for making a pattern for the tie sections, a pencil, pins, scissors, an iron, a sewing machine and, of course, an assortment of old ties.

Cutting the Ties

Remove the stitches from the back seam of each tie and take out the interlining and lining. Press the tie flat, using a damp pressing cloth to avoid harming the delicate fabrics. Lay the pattern on the wrong side of each tie and cut along the cutting line.

12: Ties should be spaced at even intervals and arranged so the narrow sections are at the waist, the wider sections at the hemline.

Sewing Ties to Skirt Fabric

Working from your skirt pattern, cut out the front and back pieces. The skirt will fit better if the major pattern sections are first cut out of the skirt fabric, and then each section is cut into wedges to accommodate the ties. Though this involves altering the tie pattern to cut proper-size skirt wedges and quite a bit of piecing, it is much easier to plan the placement of the ties on a full section of the skirt.

After you have cut out your skirt front and back, lay the ties on the fabric until you like the arrangement. Cut ½ inch off each side of the paper tie pattern. Working on the wrong side of the skirt sections, place this narrower paper pattern where you want each tie to go and draw around it with a hard pencil to mark the

1¾″

40″

3″

B
Figure B: The measurements given here include a ¼-inch seam allowance and are for ties used for the skirt pictured. Adjust the measurements to suit the garment you are making and your height. Then make a pattern and place it successively on top of each fully opened tie. Cut each tie along the cutting line.

cutting line. After marking all the wedges, cut the skirt fabric apart one wedge at a time, following the cutting lines.

Pin each tie to the skirt with right sides facing; then machine-sew the ties to the fabric. Each seam allowance should be ¼ inch. After all the ties are sewn in place, finish the skirt as your pattern directs.

The skirt shown here has a self-binding hem—a thin strip of material finishing the skirt's bottom edge—instead of the usual turned-up hem. This is made with a 1-inch strip of fabric the length of the hem. To assemble such a strip, piece sections of material cut on the bias until you have a strip of fabric the length of the hem. Place it on the skirt with right sides facing. Machine-sew the strip to the skirt, making a ¼-inch seam.

Now turn the free edge of the hem strip under ¼ inch and press it. Flip the strip to the underside of the skirt, pin it in place, and sew with a slipstitch. This hem gives the skirt an attractive edge and a professionally-finished look.

13: This is how the underside of the skirt looks with a tie strip sewn in. Press the seams toward the tie for a smoother fit.

CRAFTNOTES: TYING A TIE

These are three basic tie knots, drawn and described as if you were looking in the mirror.

Your left in the mirror.   **Your right in the mirror.**

Four-in-hand
The wide end is reflected on your right, extending about 12 inches below the narrow end.

Cross the wide end over the narrow and back underneath.

Continue around, passing the wide end across the front of the narrow end once more.

Bring the wide end up through the neck loop.

Pull the wide end down through the front loop, then tighten the knot.

Windsor
The wide end is reflected on your right, extending about 12 inches below the narrow end.

Cross the wide end over the narrow and bring it up through the neck loop.

Bring the wide end down, around, and behind the narrow end, then up on your right.

Pull the wide end back through the neck loop and across the narrow end.

Turn the wide end and pass it up through the neck loop.

Slip the wide end through the front loop and tighten the knot.

Half-Windsor
The wide end is reflected on your right, extending about 12 inches below the narrow end.

Cross the wide end over the narrow end and turn it back underneath.

Bring the wide end up through the neck loop.

Pass the wide end around the front of the tie.

Bring the wide end up through the neck loop.

Slip the wide end down through the front loop and tighten the knot.

NEEDLEPOINT
A Stitch in Time

Although Ella Projansky embroidered as a child, she became interested in needlepoint only a few years ago. Not satisfied with commercial needlepoint designs then available, she designed her own. A shop proprietor liked them and asked her to design for the shop. Mrs. Projansky did custom designing for several years before deciding to open her own studio and showroom, needlepoint things unlimited, in White Plains, New York. Mrs. Projansky teaches needlepoint at Craftsmen Unlimited in Bedford Hills, New York, at continuing education classes in Chappaqua, New York and at her studio when she is not designing for ella projansky's needleworks, inc., a mail-order business.

Needlepoint, a form of needlework that was popular in the sixteenth century, is much in vogue again—and for good reasons. Among them are needlepoint's portability, the beauty of readily available materials, the great fun to be discovered in creating an attractive design with your own stitches, and the enormous range of practical applications. Needlepoint, no longer limited to filling in the background of a pre-worked floral motif, has gained recognition as a modern, adaptable, creative form of graphic art.

What Is Needlepoint?

Basically, needlepoint is a method of completely covering an open-weave fabric with yarn. The fabric is called canvas and there are two types—mono-canvas, made with single horizontal threads crossed by single vertical threads, and penelope canvas, which has pairs of horizontal threads crossed by two closely woven vertical threads. Both come in tan or white. White is usually considered easier on the eyes for marking and counting, but use whichever you think more comfortable. The size or gauge of needlepoint canvas is designated by the number of meshes per inch (photograph 1). A mesh is one intersection of horizontal and vertical threads. The basic needlepoint stitch (Craftnotes, page 1325) is worked over one mesh. A 10-mesh canvas, for example, has 10 mesh to the inch, hence 10 stitches to the inch. The fewer mesh to the inch, the larger the stitches become, so fewer stitches are needed to cover a given area. When there are more mesh to the inch, stitches are smaller, and more are needed to cover the canvas. Mono-canvas is available with 10, 12, 14, 16, 18, 20 or 24 mesh to the inch. Penelope canvas is described with numbers, such as 10/20; the first represents the number of mesh to the inch if a pair of canvas threads are treated as one, and the second represents the number of mesh if the canvas threads are worked separately. Small stitches dividing such pairs of threads are called petit point. The most commonly used sizes of penelope canvas are 10/20, 11/22, 12/24, and 14/28. It also comes in 3½, 4 and 5 mesh- the rug canvases. In rugs the double threads are usually not separated as for petit point but are used double to give strength to the widely spaced mesh.

At one time canvas was made of linen, hemp and even silk, but today only cotton is used. The consistently high quality of canvas made in France makes it superior to other canvas. It costs more, but it is not a good idea to economize on needlepoint materials; poorly made canvas tears at the wool, and the limp threads that result make uneven stitches. The hours of work that you put into a needlepoint project and the years of enjoyment you will have from the finished product make quality materials worthwhile.

1: Canvas, the loosely woven fabric on which needlepoint is worked, comes in a variety of sizes designated by the number of mesh (intersections) per inch. From top to bottom above, pictured actual size, are 18-mesh canvas, 14-mesh canvas, 12-mesh canvas, 10-mesh canvas, and 5-mesh penelope (double-thread) canvas. The latter is also known as rug canvas.

A monogrammed pencil holder keeps pencils and markers neatly at hand in Mrs. Projansky's work area, which is backed by a splendid array of Persian yarn. For this craftswoman, the great range of colors in the raw materials serves as an inspiration for new needlepoint designs.

2: Depending on the mesh of the canvas selected, different weights of yarn are used. Shown above from left to right are two-ply Persian yarn, three-ply Persian yarn, and rug yarn.

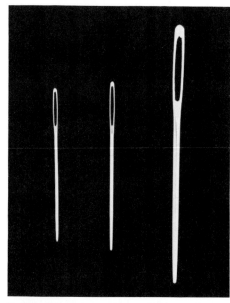

3: Among tapestry needles available are, from left to right, a No. 20 needle, used for two-ply Persian yarn, a No. 18 needle, used for three-ply Persian yarn, and a Smyrna or rug needle, used for heavy-weight rug yarn.

Other Materials

Yarn used for needlepoint must be strong enough to withstand the wear-and-tear of being pulled repeatedly through the canvas openings and still look beautiful when the needlepoint is finished. Knitting wool does not work because it is too elastic (an advantage in knitting but not in needlepoint) and because it is made of short fibers that fray quickly. Yarn used for needlepoint must have long fibers; there are several that work well. Persian wool is a loosely twisted three-ply yarn (photograph 2). Each ply is made of two strands twisted together; the plies can be used separately or together. As a three-ply yarn, Persian wool covers 10-mesh canvas well; two plies are suitable for 12- or 14-mesh canvas. Tapestry wool is a single-ply yarn made of strands more tightly twisted; they cannot be separated easily for use in a fine-mesh canvas, but the yarn is fine for 10-, 12- or 14-mesh canvas. Crewel wool, a fine embroidery yarn, is made of two strands tightly twisted together; it is used primarily for 16-mesh or smaller mesh canvas, but several strands can be used as one for working larger mesh. Rug wool is a thick, three-ply, rough-textured wool that covers large-mesh canvas quickly. Cotton, silk, rayon, and metallic threads can be used to add interest to a needlepoint work but are best confined to small areas to provide highlights since they do not wear as well as wool.

Tapestry needles—long-eyed needles with blunt points that do not split the yarn or the canvas—are used for needlepoint (photograph 3). They range in size from a No. 13 needle, the largest, to No. 24, the smallest. The eye of the needle should be slightly wider than the yarn is thick, but slim enough to slide easily through the canvas openings. A No. 18 tapestry needle works best for 10- and 12-mesh canvas, a No. 19 or 20 for 14-mesh canvas, and a No. 24 needle for 24-mesh canvas. A No. 13 needle (also known as a rug needle) is used with rug yarn on large-mesh canvas.

In addition to canvas, yarn, and needles, you will need: a tape measure or ruler for measuring the canvas; small, sharp scissors for cutting yarn and stitches; large shears for cutting canvas; graph paper for working out designs; a fine-tip, water-proof marker for marking guidelines and the center of the canvas; and 1-inch-wide masking tape for binding edges. If you use a thimble for other needlework, you will probably want to use it for needlepoint.

Preparing the Canvas

Canvas is sold by the yard, or fraction of a yard, and is available in widths from 18 to 60 inches. To determine the size of the canvas you need, add 2 inches to each side of the finished project for the seam allowance and blocking (squaring up the work). Cut the canvas, and fold strips of masking tape over the raw edges to keep the canvas threads from raveling or catching at the yarn. Selvage edges do not need to be bound with tape.

There are two ways of marking a needlepoint design on the canvas; you can plot each stitch on a graph-paper chart, or you can paint the design directly on the canvas. Graphing is most suitable for geometric designs, lettering, and repeat patterns. Each square on the graph will equal one stitch on the canvas (Figure D, page 1323); the needlepoint is worked by counting the squares on the graph and working that number of stitches on the canvas. Painting the canvas is a good technique for more intricate designs; it gives you an accurate guide right on the canvas. If you have chosen a design that you would like enlarged or reduced, you can take the picture to a shop that makes photostats (they are listed in the Yellow Pages) and have a positive stat made that is exactly the size you want.

To transfer any design on the canvas, put the canvas over the pattern, and outline the major areas with a waterproof marker. To fill in the color, use a waterproof medium because the canvas will be dampened for blocking, and a water-soluble color might run and stain the wool. Oil paints and acrylic paints can be used since both are waterproof, but felt-tipped markers are easiest to use. Check them first, however; water-resistant does not mean waterproof. Color a small piece of canvas with the marker, let it dry, wet it, and rub it. If the color comes off on your finger, it will ruin the finished needlepoint. If you only have markers that are not waterproof, spray the canvas with an acrylic fixitive before you start to stitch. It is not necessary to color an area completely; a piece of yarn tied to the area will serve as a color reminder.

Stitching

For stitching, thread the needle (Figure A) with a length of yarn. Do not knot the yarn. Put the needle through from the front of the canvas about an inch from the place where you want the first stitch to be. Hold the yarn in place behind the canvas. As you work the first stitches, catch the end of yarn in the back so it will be secured (photograph 4). (The end that sticks out in front will later be snipped off in back.) To end a length of yarn, run the needle through the back of the stitches for about an inch (photograph 5), and snip the yarn off close to the stitches. Start and end all subsequent yarn lengths by weaving the needle under the stitches horizontally or vertically. When making stitches, work gently, allowing the yarn to rest on the canvas threads without being pulled taut. The yarn may become twisted as you work. If this happens, let it drop freely from the canvas, and it will untwist itself.

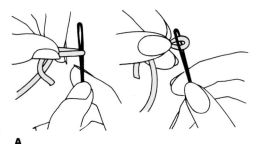

A

Figure A: To thread a tapestry needle, fold one inch of yarn over the needle and pull taut (left). Pinch this fold with the thumb and forefinger, slip it off the needle, and push the pinched fold through the eye of the needle (right).

4: To start the yarn, put the needle and yarn through the canvas from the front, about an inch from where you will make the first stitch. As you work the first stitches, catch the yarn on the back so it will be secured.

5: To end a length of yarn, thread it through stitches on the back of the canvas for about an inch horizontally or vertically, not diagonally. The stitches will hold the yarn; cut off any yarn that is left over.

Blocking

Blocking is done to smooth and straighten a finished needlepoint canvas that may have been stretched or pulled out of shape during the stitching. You will need rustproof push-pins or tacks; a ¾-inch-thick piece of plywood or insulation board that is larger than the worked needlepoint; brown wrapping paper; aluminum foil; a waterproof marker; a ruler; a T-square or right-angle; and a towel. Cover the board with aluminum foil to protect it. Place the brown wrapping paper on top of this. Using the waterproof marker, draw a rectangle the size that the finished needlepoint should be. Mark the center of each side on the paper and on the needlepoint. The needlepoint can be washed at the same time as it is blocked. Soak it in cold-water soap and water for 3 minutes. Rinse until the water is clear; do not wring. Roll tightly in a towel until excess water is absorbed. Place the worked needlepoint face down if it is tent stitches, face up if it is decorative stitches, on the paper-covered board. The two-inch border of canvas that was included in the original measurement of the canvas is used now for tacking. Tacks should not go into worked needlepoint.

Your objective is to line up the needlepoint with the outline. Tack at the center of the top and bottom; then tack the center of each side, stretching the needlepoint as necessary to fit the marked outline. Check the corners with the square or right-angle. Continue stretching and tacking opposite points around the work until the entire border is tacked at one-inch intervals. Keep the board flat to avoid sagging. Let it dry thoroughly—at least 24 hours, and up to three days if the air is humid. Then you can remove the tacks, and protect it with spray-on stain repellent.

Frames

Many experienced needlepointers like to use a frame because it holds the canvas taut, making the stitching go faster and more smoothly. The taut canvas also makes counting threads easier. The part of the canvas not being worked is kept rolled up and stays clean. However, most lap frames are not particularly portable and are cumbersome for the needle-pointer who likes to carry work around. Floor frames are a great convenience for the needlepointer who wants to work in the comfort of home. Frames are essential for rug making because the frame helps support the weight of the rug canvas. For any other needlepoint project, the use of a frame is optional. Directions for mounting the canvas come with the frame.

Opportunities are unlimited for personalizing in needlepoint; start with a monogram and you will soon be creating your own designs.

Gingham pencil holder

$ ▨ 👫 🐿

Making a monogrammed pencil holder will give you a personal yet simple introduction to needlepoint. It uses only variations of the basic needlepoint stitch—the tent stitch—as detailed in the Craftnotes on page 1325. To cover an 18-ounce can, you will need a 14-by-8-inch piece of 10-mesh canvas and three-ply Persian yarn in the following amounts: 20 yards of light blue; 13 yards of dark blue; 11 yards of white; 4 yards of red; and 1 yard of black. Cut your canvas to size, and bind the edges with masking tape to protect the yarn and prevent raveling. Draw the outline of the finished needlepoint—10 inches by 4⅛ inches for the 18-ounce can—on the canvas with a marker. (If you prefer a can of a different size, measure height and circumference, and add at least 4 inches to each dimension to get the size of the canvas needed.) Measure and mark the center of the outlined needlepoint area (Figure D); this is where you will center the middle initial if you are using three initials. If you use only two initials, place them on either side of the center mark. Next, draw a horizontal line about 2½ inches long through the center point, and place the body of the letters on this line letting the descending parts of the letters go below the line as necessary. This places the initials slightly above the center of the worked needlepoint, and makes the ladybug more visible.

Thread a No. 20 needle with an 18-inch length of red yarn using only two of the three plies, and make your initials with the continental stitch following the alphabet in Figure D. Then, continuing with two plies of yarn and using the basket weave stitch, fill in the ladybug following the graph pattern also in Figure D. Next, fill in the gingham background, again using the basket weave stitch. Finally, make the red border with one row of the continental stitch. When the needlepoint is complete, block the canvas, following the directions on page 1321.

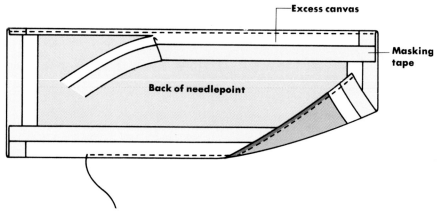

B

Figure B: Fold the excess canvas on the top and bottom to the wrong side, and stitch between the first and second rows of needlepoint stitches; trim to within ¼ inch of the folds and sides.

To finish the work, fold back the excess canvas at the top and bottom, and machine-stitch it between the red border row and the first blue row (Figure B). (If you are sewing by hand, use carpet thread, a strong, waxed cotton thread.) Cut off excess canvas ¼ inch from the stitching. Except for a ¼-inch allowance on each side, trim the excess canvas from the sides. Fold the allowance back. Fit the needlepoint onto the can, and stitch the two edges of canvas together where they meet (Figure C) using a cross stitch with the top stroke going from lower left to upper right (Craftnotes page 1326). Put a 3-inch circle of felt, cork, or cardboard inside the can to protect the pen and pencil points.

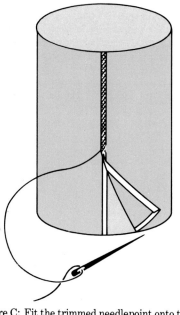

C

Figure C: Fit the trimmed needlepoint onto the can, and fold back the ¼-inch allowance at the sides. Close the seam with a cross stitch (Craftnotes, page 1326).

Figure D: You can use appropriate letters from the alphabet opposite to make any needlepoint monogram or name. Each square represents one stitch on the canvas. To position initials on the gingham pattern (upper right), draw a horizontal line through the center point. Let the body of the initials rest on this line with only descenders going below.

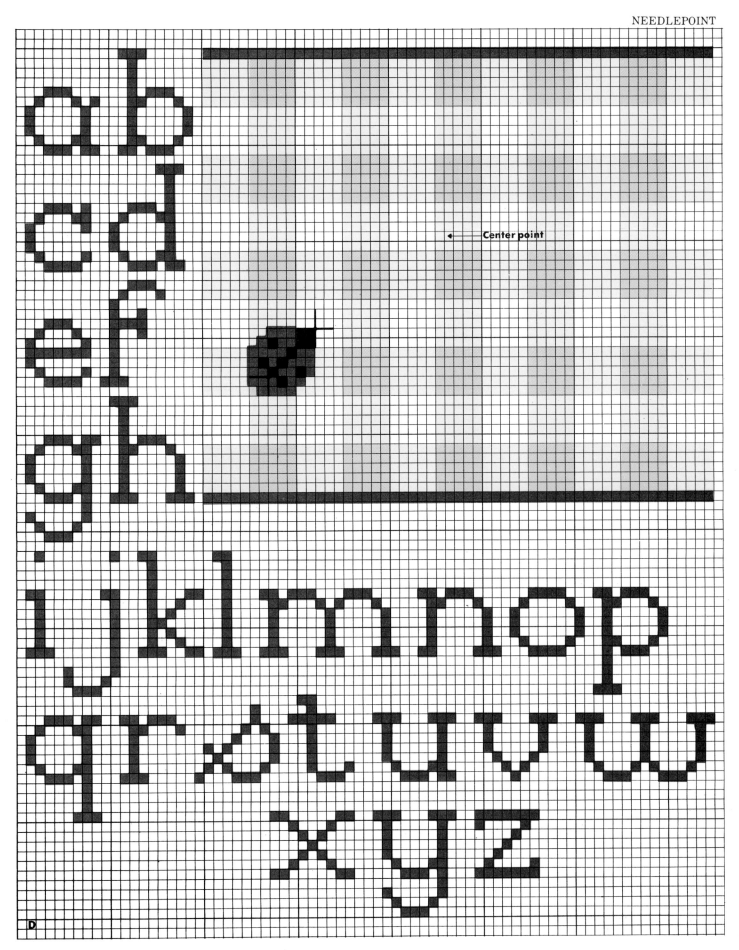

Center point

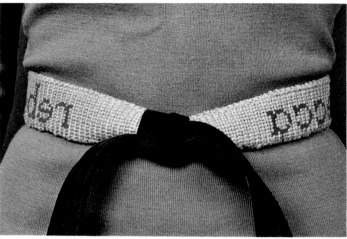

Rebecca's name is clearly readable on the back of the belt (left), while the mirror-image names on the sides of the belt make an interesting design (right).

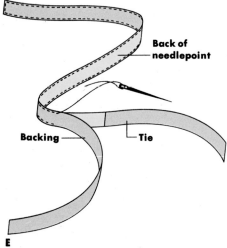

Figure E: With the right sides facing, stitch the backing fabric to the needlework belt and its ties, making small stitches by hand.

Labels in Figure E: Back of needlepoint — Backing — Tie — E

Needlecrafts
Signature belt

A belt signed in needlepoint lets you wear your handwork and get credit for it at the same time. The name is centered on the back of the belt, and mirror images of the name are stitched on either side. The background is worked in the reverse tent stitch (see Craftnotes, page 1326) to give it more texture, and the name is worked in the continental stitch using the alphabet letters in Figure D (page 1323). To make the belt, you will need less than ¼ yard of 10-mesh canvas (perhaps a piece left over from another project); three-ply Persian yarn—3 yards of rose for the name, 6 yards of red for the two mirror-image names, and enough beige for the background; and approximately ¼ yard of 36-inch-wide imitation suede cloth for the belt's backing and ties. To figure the amount of yarn needed for the background, measure your waist, and multiply that measurement by 2½; the reverse tent stitch requires 2½ yards of yarn for each running inch that is 1¾ inches wide. The belt pictured is 25 inches long and required 62½ yards of three-ply Persian yarn. If your name is a long one, or has more tall letters, add 1 yard of yarn to the amount specified for each name.

The finished needlepoint will be 1¾ inches wide. Cut a strip of 10-mesh canvas 5¾ inches wide (the width of the needlepoint plus a 2-inch margin on each side) and the length of your waist measurement plus a 2-inch margin on each end. Bind the edges with masking tape.

To stitch the name, center the middle letter in the middle of the belt. Complete the name. To work the mirror-image names on either side, hold the belt up to the mirror, and copy the letters as they appear in the image. (If you prefer, you could repeat the name three times without reversing it.) When the names are complete, fill in the background with the reverse tent stitch. Block the needlepoint following the directions on page 1321. Trim the excess canvas to a ½-inch border all around.

To make the backing, cut four 2¾-inch-wide strips (1¾ inches for the belt width plus a ½-inch seam allowance on either side) from the imitation suede cloth. Sew an 18-inch-long strip to each end of the needlepoint for the ties using a sewing machine or making small stitches by hand (Figure E). Sew two strips together to make whatever length of backing you need (the length of the needlepoint plus the length of the two ties). Place the needlepoint and the long backing strip with the right sides facing, and stitch them together ½ inch from the edge leaving only the last three inches open so the belt can be turned right-side out. Make sure the machine stitches go between the last 2 rows of needlepoint stitches so the excess canvas does not show. Turn the belt and press it. Using small hand stitches, sew the opening closed. With a sewing machine, top stitch around the entire belt—both the needlepoint and the fabric ties—¼ inch from the edges; the belt is ready to wear.

CRAFTNOTES: THE BASIC NEEDLEPOINT STITCH

The basic needlepoint stitch is called the tent stitch. The name comes from the Middle English word **tenter** which meant a stretching implement or frame, similar to the frame on which needlepoint was then worked. The smallest unit in needlepoint, the tent stitch, is a flat, even stitch covering just one intersection of canvas threads. Every tent stitch slants in the same direction—from lower left to upper right—so every tent stitch is identical.

But there are several variations in the making of tent stitches. Although the stitches look identical from the front of the canvas, how they are made determines what they will look like from the back. The continental stitch is the tent stitch worked in a line, either horizontally from right to left (as illustrated); vertically from top to bottom; diagonally downward to the left or the right; or diagonally upward to the left. On the back, the continental stitch makes long slanting stitches that cover the canvas fairly well. This stitch is used primarily for outlining and is not recommended for fill-in work because it pulls the canvas out of shape.

The basket weave variation is worked diagonally and gets its name from the woven pattern that appears on the reverse side; the direction of the work is changed with each row. Since stitches that run in only one direction tend to pull the canvas askew, the basket weave variation is the best to use for filling in the canvas with tent stitches. Such stitches do not pull the canvas out of shape and actually reinforce the weave of the canvas threads. To follow the grain of canvas with basket weave stitches, it is necessary to differentiate between vertical and horizontal mesh. This is determined by the top thread of the intersection. Hence, a vertical mesh has a vertical thread on top, a horizontal mesh has a horizontal thread on top. Rows of stitches covering the vertical mesh are worked downward, from the top left to the bottom right, and rows of stitches that cover horizontal mesh are worked upward from the bottom right to the top left, thereby filling the entire area. It gives a heavy padding to the work and does not pull the canvas out of shape.

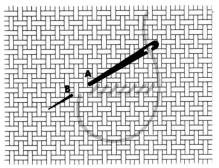

The continental: To work this variation of the tent stitch, put the needle in at A, and bring it out at B, so the yarn covers one intersection of canvas threads.

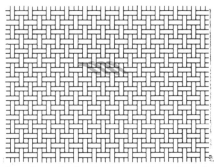

Seen from the back, the continental stitch makes long slanting stitches that cover the canvas fairly well.

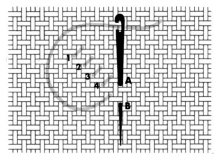

The basket weave: In this variation, rows covering vertical mesh are worked diagonally downward, the stitches made in the numbered sequence shown. Put the needle in at A, and bring it out at B so the yarn covers one vertical mesh.

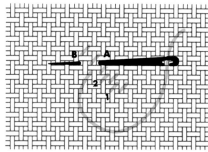

Rows covering the horizontal mesh on the basket weave variation are worked diagonally upward, the stitches made in the numbered sequence shown. Put the needle in at A, and bring it out at B so the yarn covers one horizontal mesh.

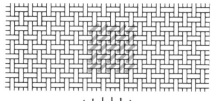

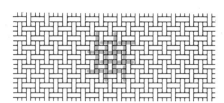

The basket weave stitch gets its name from the woven pattern that it forms on the back of the canvas.

To fill an entire area with basket weave stitches (top), work the stitches following the numbered sequence shown in the magnification (bottom).

A decorative stitch in needlepoint may cover more than one intersection of canvas threads at a time, thereby appearing to be raised, and it may go in any direction including vertical and horizontal, having been stitched across the canvas threads rather than across the intersection of those threads. Where stitches must share the same hole, the new stitch should enter from the front of the canvas, if possible, so the existing stitch is not split by the needle.

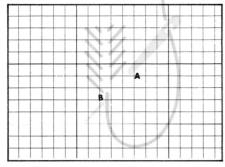

Kalem Stitch

This stitch sequence consists of two rows of diagonal stitches each over two intersections, one row with stitches slanting up to the left, and the other slanting up to the right, sharing the same center hole. Work down from the top of the row to the bottom. Put the needle in at A, and bring it out at B.

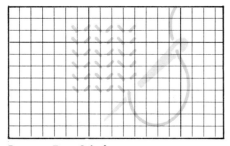

Reverse Tent Stitch

This stitch is worked the same as the Kalem stitch, but each stitch covers only one intersection.

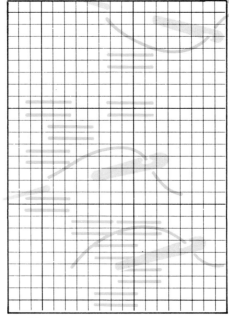

Double Brick Stitch

This stitch sequence consists of rows of two stitches over four threads, each pair of stitches staggered in bricklayer fashion. Work two stitches over four threads of the canvas, skip two spaces, work two more stitches in line with the first two. When the first row is completed (top drawing), start the second row below the top stitches in the first row, staggered two spaces to the right (center drawing). The stitches in the third row share a hole with those in the first row. Turn the canvas upside down so the needle can go into the shared hole from the front (bottom drawing).

Willow Stitch

Work the double brick stitch. With the needle threaded with another color, anchor the yarn at one side of the canvas. Twist the needle until the yarn is taut (about 10 times), and, being careful not to split the yarn of the brick stitches, run the yarn under the bricks, not under the canvas. Secure at the other side.

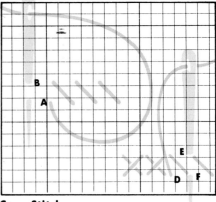

Cross Stitch

Working from right to left, bring the needle up at A and down at B (upper left), for the first stroke. Then, starting from the left bring the needle up at D, down at E, up at F to make the cross stroke (lower right).

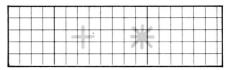

Reverse Smyrna Cross Stitch

Work an upright cross stitch over two threads (left). Over the upright cross stitch, work a diagonal cross stitch (right), with the top stroke slanting from lower right to upper left.

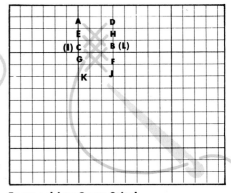

Encroaching Cross Stitch

This stitch pattern consists of cross stitches over two canvas threads, each stitch beginning in the skipped mesh of the preceding stitch. Bring the needle up at A, down at B, up at C, and down at D for the first cross stitch. Start the second stitch in the space left by the first (E). Bring the needle down at F, up at G, down at H. The third stitch shares a hole with the first; come up at I (also C), down at J, up at K, down at L (also B).

DECORATIVE STITCHES

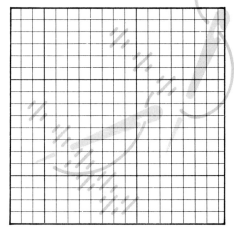

Mosaic Stitch

Worked diagonally, this stitch sequence consists of three diagonal stitches, the first over one mesh, the second over two, the third over one (upper right). In succeeding rows, the small stitches share a hole, and the long stitches are worked into the spaces that remain (lower left).

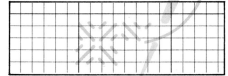

Reverse Mosaic Block

This is the mosaic stitch sequence worked into a block. The four long stitches of the block share the center hole.

Knotted Upright Cross Stitch

This sequence starts with a cross stitch over 4 threads (left). The needle is then brought up in the center hole, below the horizontal stitch and to the left of the vertical. It is brought under the vertical thread and across the intersection, then to the back of the canvas to the right of the vertical and below the horizontal stitch.

Reverse Mosaic Block with Knotted Upright Cross Stitch

The combination of the reverse mosaic block and the knotted upright cross looks like this.

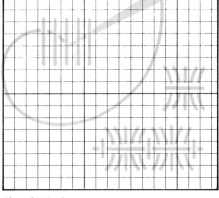

Sheaf Stitch

Make five upright stitches over four horizontal canvas threads. Bring the needle up in the middle space of the canvas behind the canvas, and slide it under the stitches to the left and out (top). Bringing the needle across the stitches to the right, return the needle to the middle space behind the stitches and pull taut (center). Sheaf stitches share top and bottom holes at the start and finish of each unit. An upright cross stitch between sheaves completes the pattern (bottom).

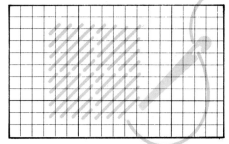

Scotch Stitch

This stitch sequence of graduated diagonal stitches forms a square. Starting at a corner, the first stitch should cover one mesh. Succeeding stitches cover two, three, four, three, two, and one mesh. All stitches slant in the same direction, from lower left to upper right.

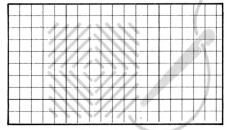

Reverse Scotch Stitch

This is worked the same as the Scotch stitch above, but with adjacent units slanting in opposite directions.

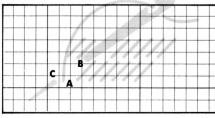

Oblique Gobelin Stitch

This stitch sequence is formed of rows of stitches that cover the same number of canvas threads (from two to six). Bring the needle up at A, down at B, up at C. The top of one row and the bottom of the next row share a hole. This stitch may be worked horizontally or vertically.

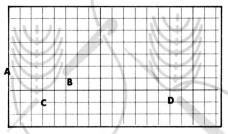

Fly Stitch

This stitch must be worked from the top of the row to the bottom. Bring the needle up at A, down at B, up in the center at C, down again at D. Repeat for each stitch. Use small slanting stitches as necessary to fill in at the beginning and end of each row.

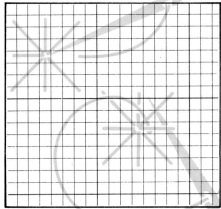

Small Whipped Spider Web

Use a long strand of yarn, and make eight spokes that share a center hole and form a square (top). Bring the needle out to the front as close as possible to the center. Carry the yarn under two spokes and back over one (bottom). Continue around until all eight spokes are completely covered, giving corner spokes one or two extra wraps of yarn.

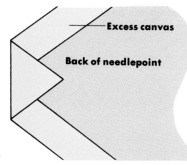

F
Figure F: After cutting the border edges of canvas to the same width, start mitering a corner by folding the point toward the center of the back of the canvas so the fold line is at the corner stitch of the needlepoint.

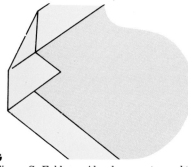

G
Figure G: Fold one side edge over toward the center of the board so that the excess canvas does not show on the front of the needlepoint.

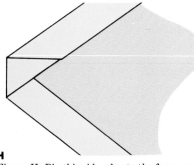

H
Figure H: Pin this side edge to the foam-core board to keep it in place.

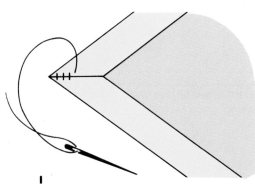

I
Figure I: Fold the other side; stitch the diagonal seam at the corner, unraveling a thread from leftover canvas to use for sewing.

A simple mirror (available at variety stores) becomes an important room accessory when framed with a 2½-inch-wide needlepoint design.

Needlecrafts
Frame yourself

$ ▯ ☗ ☒

What prettier way is there to see yourself than framed in needlepoint? To make a mirror frame, you will need: ½ yard of 10-mesh canvas; three-ply Persian yarn in the following amounts—79 yards of pink, 15½ yards of purple, and 8½ yards of red; a 5-inch-square unframed mirror (available at variety and department stores); a 9-inch-square of foam-core board (available at art supply stores); a 9-inch-square piece of felt in a harmonious color; and white glue.

The Willow Stitch Border
The frame is worked in the willow stitch which is made by weaving twisted yarn into a double brick stitch background (see Craftnotes, page 1326). Cut a piece of canvas 13 inches square and bind the edges with masking tape. Measure to locate a 5-inch square in the center and mark its outline with a marker. This area is left blank; when the needlepoint is finished, the mirror will be glued here. Work the double brick stitch background 24 threads wide around the 5-inch square. Around this, work four rows of the continental stitch. The yarn that is worked into the double brick stitches to make the willow stitch is woven in this order: one pink, one red, one pink, five purple. Repeat this six times down the frame; then end with one pink, one red, and one pink. Block the needlepoint; do not trim the excess canvas.

To make the frame rigid, put white glue on the back of the 5-inch-square of empty canvas, and center it on the 9-inch-square of foam-core board, thus gluing it in place. Miter the corners of the canvas around the back of the foam-core board (Figures F, G, H and I). Secure the canvas to the board by lacing the canvas edges together (Figure J) starting from the center of opposite sides and working toward the right. Then turn the canvas around, and lace the other half from the center to the right. Repeat for the sides. When the lacing is complete, take the tape off the edges of the canvas. The adhesive that remains will help keep the sewing threads in place. The outside four rows of continental stitches should cover the sides of the foam-core board which is about ⅜ inch thick. Put glue on the empty canvas and on the back of the mirror, and glue the mirror in place. Cover the mirror with a piece of paper; then weight it down with a telephone book or brick until the glue dries.

Making Twisted Cords

To give a finishing touch to the mirror, make twisted cords in red and purple to border the mirror, and one in pink to border the frame. To estimate the amount of yarn needed for each color of cord, allow three times the circumference multiplied by the number of strands used. Thus, for the red and purple cords, the circumference of the 5-inch mirror is 20 inches, times three is 60 inches, times the two strands used is 120 inches, or approximately 3½ yards of each color. The pink cord, which goes around the 9-inch-square frame, is twice as thick. The circumference is 36 inches, times three is 108 inches, times the four strands used is 432 inches, or 12 yards. (These yarn amounts are included in the yarn estimates given above.)

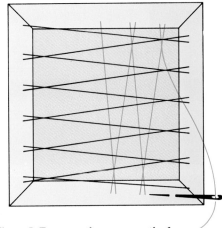

J
Figure J: To secure the canvas on the foam-core board, lace opposite edges of the border together on the back, starting at the center and working toward the right, then turn the canvas around and lace the other half from the center to the right.

K
Figure K: It takes two people to make a twisted cord; each ties the ends of two strands of yarn to a pencil with a slip knot and twists the pencil clockwise until the strands are completely twisted.

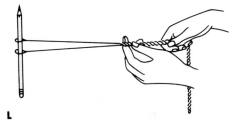

L
Figure L: As your partner holds the pencil, free the looped center and slide one hand down the yarn, stopping at short intervals to let the yarn below your hand twist by itself. When you reach the pencil, tie each end with a bit of yarn below the knot; then untie the knots.

Making a twisted cord requires two people. For the red and purple cords, cut the 3½ yards of yarn in half. Keep the two strands together, and tie each end to a pencil using a slipknot. To keep the yarn taut, each person should hold it just below the pencil with one hand, and twist the pencil clockwise with the other (Figure K). Both people must twist the pencil clockwise. When the entire length of yarn is twisted, loop the middle over a door knob or chair spindle. Bring the two pencils together, and slip both loops onto one pencil. While one person holds the pencil, the other takes the yarn by the center thus folding it in half. This person slides one hand down the yarn, releasing it at short intervals and letting the yarn twist by itself (Figure L). Once this is done for the entire length, a bit of yarn tied below the slipknots will secure the twist so the pencil can be removed and the slipknots untied.

The pink cord is made the same way but is twice as thick. Cut the 12 yards of yarn into quarters. Take the four strands and make a twisted cord as described above.

To sew the red and purple cords onto the mirror, use 2 plies of yarn in the same color and a sewing needle. Find the center of the purple twisted cord, and stitch this to the upper left corner of the mirror. Sew half of the cord along the top and down the right side of the mirror; sew the other half down the left side and across the bottom. The cords will meet at the bottom right corner. Tie them together, and separate the plies to make fringe. Repeat for the red cord. The pink cord is sewn onto the edge of the frame in the same way, but when the two halves meet at the lower right corner, overlap them slightly and tack the ends to the back of the frame stitching them to the canvas. To make the back of the frame neat, cut a piece of felt 9 inches square, and stitch it to the last row of continental stitch on all four edges.

Needlecrafts
A stitchery pillow

The pillow cover pictured opposite incorporates many different decorative needlepoint stitches. Although it is large—14 inches square—the pillow cover works up quickly because it is made with rug yarn on 5-mesh rug canvas. To make the pillow, you will need: an 18-inch-square piece of the rug canvas; eight ounces of a good wool rug yarn for the pillow front; two ounces of rug yarn for the tassels; a rug needle; ½ yard of backing fabric color-coordinated with the pillow; and a 14-inch knife-edge pillow form. It is important to use good yarn because the beauty of the pillow depends on the sculptured look of the decorative stitches; the yarn must be soft, yet firm enough to hold the shape of the stitch.

The geometric design of the pillow lends itself to graph-paper representation. (Figure M shows the upper left-hand quarter of the design.) Each line on the graph represents one thread in the canvas. Thus, there is no need to mark the placement of stitches on the canvas itself; simply refer to the graph and count threads.

First, cut the canvas to unfinished size—an 18-inch-square—and bind the edges with masking tape. Mark the outline of the center of the canvas and the 14-inch square with a marker. Start the center stitch unit—a reverse mosaic block (see Craftnotes, pages 1326 and 1327). The four long stitches should come together in

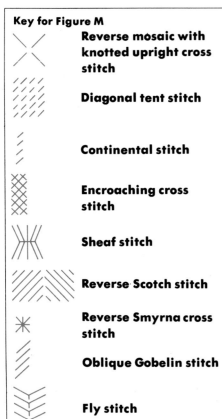

Key for Figure M

Reverse mosaic with knotted upright cross stitch

Diagonal tent stitch

Continental stitch

Encroaching cross stitch

Sheaf stitch

Reverse Scotch stitch

Reverse Smyrna cross stitch

Oblique Gobelin stitch

Fly stitch

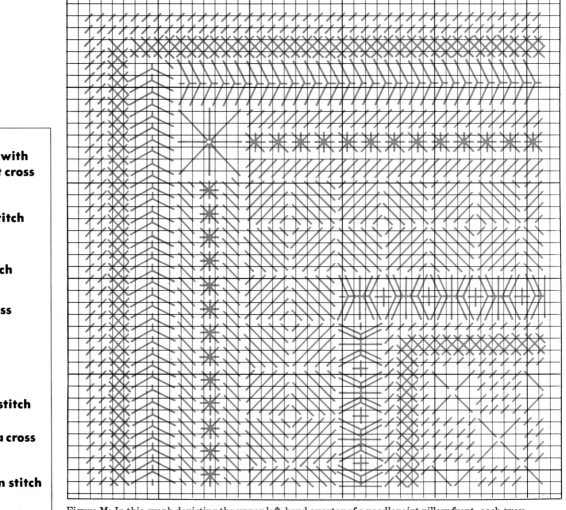

Figure M: In this graph depicting the upper left-hand quarter of a needlepoint pillow front, each grey line represents a canvas thread. The stitch representations show the placement of various stitches described in the Craftnotes, (pages 1326 and 1327). To follow this graph, simply count the squares and match the totals on your canvas.

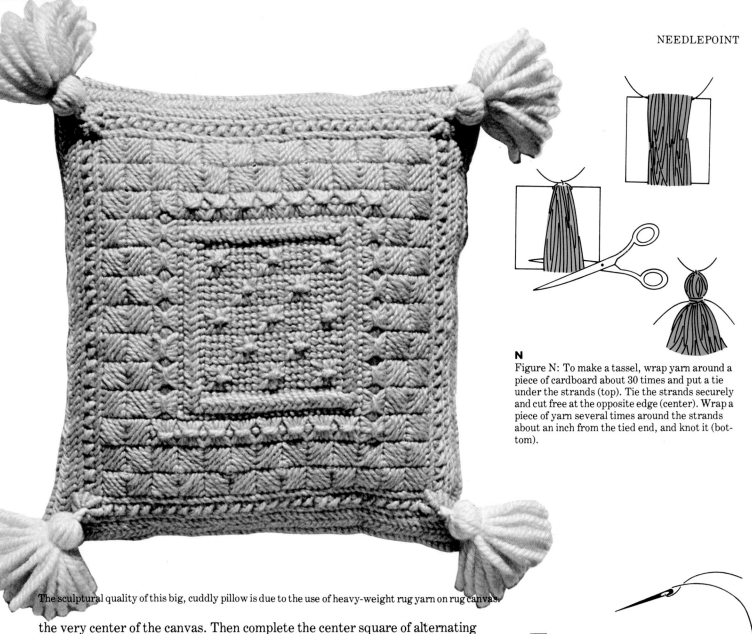

The sculptural quality of this big, cuddly pillow is due to the use of heavy-weight rug yarn on rug canvas.

N

Figure N: To make a tassel, wrap yarn around a piece of cardboard about 30 times and put a tie under the strands (top). Tie the strands securely and cut free at the opposite edge (center). Wrap a piece of yarn several times around the strands about an inch from the tied end, and knot it (bottom).

the very center of the canvas. Then complete the center square of alternating reverse mosaic blocks and diagonal tent stitches. Now work each succeeding row around this center square, referring to the graph (Figure M) for the placement of the stitches, and to the Craftnotes for how to make the stitch. The last two rows of the continental stitch act as a seam allowance for the design area. When the needlepoint is complete, block it, following the directions on page 1321.

To make the pillow tassels, first cut a piece of cardboard 3½ inches wide and wrap yarn around it about 30 times. Slip a 6-inch-long piece of yarn under the strands (Figure N), and tie it tightly at one edge gathering the strands together. Cut the strands free at the opposite edge of the cardboard. Wrap another piece of yarn several times around the strands about 1 inch from the tied end, knot it, and trim the tassel ends. Thread the top tie yarn through a rug needle, and use it to sew the tassel to the center of a whipped spider-web stitch on one of the corners of the pillow. Repeat for the other corners.

To complete the pillow, cut a 15-inch square of backing fabric, and trim the canvas surrounding the worked and blocked needlepoint leaving a ½-inch border. With right sides facing, pin and baste the needlepoint to the backing fabric, keeping the edges of both pieces even. Sew the two together around three sides, including all four corners, using a sewing machine or making small stitches by hand (Figure O) and taking care to stitch only into the two extra rows of continental stitches. Turn the pillow cover right side out and insert the pillow form. On the opening, fold the raw edges of the needlepoint canvas and the backing fabric to the inside, and sew them together with tiny stitches.

O

Figure O: With right sides facing, stitch the needlepoint to the pillow backing by sewing along three sides and all four corners, leaving a 10-inch opening. Trim the corners, then turn the pillow cover right side out. Insert the pillow form and close the opening with tiny stitches.

A commercially-made acrylic shag rug is given a new look with a needlepointed border that has been sewn onto a shaved area of the rug.

A needlepoint rug

Many experienced needlepointers yearn to make a needlepoint rug that might become a family heirloom but shy away from what they imagine to be an enormous project. To needlepoint an entire rug, even a small one, is, indeed, a time-consuming undertaking. The rug pictured above, however, is an ingenious combination of needlepoint with a commercially-made acrylic shag rug. It gives you much of the satisfaction of making a needlepoint rug without all that work.

For this project, you will need: a 2-by-3-foot rug with a jute or burlap backing (avoid latex as it is difficult to sew through); ¾ yard of 36-inch-wide heavy cotton or lightweight burlap for lining; and carpet thread (a heavy-duty sewing thread) to attach the lining. (The commercially-made scatter rug that is sold as a 2-by-3-foot rug actually measures 23 by 34 inches.) To make the needlepoint border, you will need: ¾ yard of 36-inch-wide 10-mesh canvas; approximately 500 yards of three-ply Persian yarn; and a No. 18 tapestry needle. To estimate the amount of yarn needed in each color, allow half the total amount, 250 yards, for the background color, and divide the remaining yarn by the number of colors used in the pattern. The rug pictured above was worked in four shades of lavender and two of green; it required approximately 42 yards of each of the six design colors plus 250 yards of beige for the background.

Figure P: This needlepoint design fits along one long side and two short sides of the rug. The other long side is simply a repeat of the design for the long side given here.

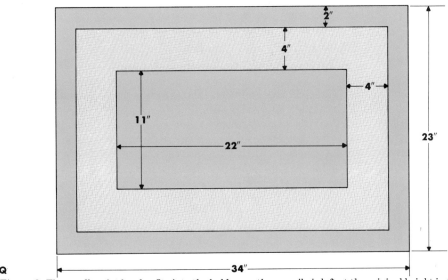

Q

Figure Q: The needlepoint border fits into the bald area; the rug pile is left at the original height in the center rectangle and along the 2-inch-wide outside border.

To avoid counting stitches (difficult on an intricate floral pattern), paint the canvas following the drawing in Figure P and the directions on page 1320. The rug is made in two steps: first the needlepoint is worked on a piece of canvas; then it is sewn to the shag rug. The finished needlepoint makes a 4-inch-wide border, measuring 19 by 30 inches on its outer edge. Do not cut out the blank canvas in the center of the design until the needlepoint work is completed and blocked. To do the needlepoint, outline the butterfly and leaf shapes with the continental stitch, and fill them in with the basket weave stitch; then fill in the background with the basket weave stitch. Block the completed needlepoint following the directions on page 1321. Then cut away the excess canvas allowing a 2-inch border inside and outside the worked area. Fold back this excess canvas, and miter the corners (see Figures F, G, H and I).

To prepare the shag rug for its new border, mark the 4-inch-wide border where the needlepoint will go, leaving a 2-inch-wide border of shag (Figure Q). Cut the shag down to the rug backing in this 4-inch-wide area with a pair of scissors. To get this area as flat as possible, use an old safety razor with a new blade to shave the remaining stubble. Place the needlepoint border in this bald area, and stitch the last row of needlepoint stitches to the rug backing, using heavy-duty sewing thread and making small stitches by hand. To make a lining to protect the rug, cut a piece of lining fabric 24 by 35 inches (the rug measurement plus ½ inch on each side for a seam allowance). Fold under the seam allowance, and press with a steam iron. Pin the lining to the back of the rug, and sew around the entire rug using the heavy-duty sewing thread and making small stitches by hand.

For related entries, see "Crewelwork Sampler," "Embroidery," "Florentine Stitch."

Anthony Toney, teacher and artist, is the author of Creative Painting and Drawing. *His work is exhibited at the ACA Gallery in New York. He has won awards and is a member of the National Academy of Design, Audubon Artists, the Artists Equity Association, and the National Society of Mural Painters. He teaches at the New School for Social Research in New York.*

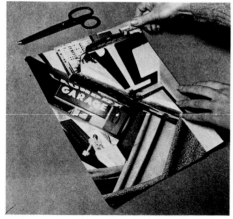

1: Color photographs clipped from an old magazine can be arranged to make a collage, giving new insights into the visual relationships of line, color, shape and texture.

These alternating stripes of red and green are of the same value (lightness or darkness) and intensity (purity or grayness). Such juxtaposed colors of the same value and intensity often seem to vibrate when you stare at them—depending on their size and shape.

OIL PAINTING
New Ways of Seeing

The painted image originated thousands upon thousands of years ago, when prehistoric man discovered its almost magical power. Those earthy artists, whose works on cave walls still survive the assault of time, used paints made from clays containing minerals. Over the centuries since, the medium has become more sophisticated as has the message. Each era has artists who discover new ways to view the world and new techniques to use in communicating that view. Yet behind all the diversity of style and method, there are some constants.

The basic elements themselves—line, space, color, texture, value and shape—do not change; they are discussed and illustrated on pages 1336 and 1337. And regardless of subject matter, there are but two major techniques used in creating an image on canvas—called direct painting and indirect painting. In the former, paint is mixed on the palette to the desired color and applied to the canvas to create an image as directly and immediately as possible (it does not have to be a photographic image, of course; it can be an image that has existed only in the artist's mind). The still life shown on page 1336 is such a direct painting. In indirect painting, the artist gradually builds up an image on the canvas, starting with highlights and shadows, then gradually adding many coats of more or less transparent color. With this method, the apple image in the still life might have been started with white brush strokes on an umber background rather than with a blob of red paint. Underpainting is illustrated in the portrait on page 1347. The permanent oil paints applied to a sheet of bond paper in the color photograph at right are rich in color and lustrous in texture; they can be dripped, blotted, scraped or brushed onto a canvas. If you are allergic to oils, try fast-drying acrylic paints.

The Creative Process
The period in which you decide what to paint—and how to paint it—is the freest part of the undertaking. For it to be fruitful, seeing the world accurately yet with fresh perception is vital. There are a number of tricks that will help you break out of perceptual habits that hinder artistic expression.

Try ripping magazine pictures into different shapes to distort images and investigate the new relationships of line, color, texture, and shape that occur when objects are taken out of a familiar context. The collage at left is an example of such an experiment. The draperies become pure texture and color juxtaposed with the smoothness of the white dress. The lettering becomes shape and mass on a blue background. The lady herself, out of proportion to the other elements, seems more an artistic whim than a human figure.

Seeing how color works is another trick for stimulating new perceptions. Different colors carry different emotional meanings, and in combination, they may give a painting an overall somber tone, shock value, restfulness or intensity. One way of experimenting is to use silk-screened paper that comes in many colors and is sold in art supply stores. In the color band at left (bottom), strips of orange and green silk-screened paper placed next to each other seem to vibrate.

Painting itself may vary in style from the most realistic representation possible to the most abstract—where an object may be distorted or not be present at all. In either case, close observation of the world around you is imperative. If you are creating a three-dimensional image on a two-dimensional surface, some understanding of perspective is essential (page 1341). Symbolism, at the other end of the scale, also requires close observation of reality—in this case to seek an abstract shape, color or line that best expresses your private reality.

How to use the various tools available to artists—paint, canvas, brushes and additives—is discussed in the Craftnotes on pages 1338 and 1339.

Oil painting is not always done with brushes. Fingers, cotton swabs, rags and palette knives were used to apply paint on the sheet of bond paper pictured opposite, to achieve a variety of textures.

The Visual Vocabulary of Painting

Line
In addition to forming shapes, line is an artistic element in its own right. Lines may be curved or straight, and may be positioned horizontally, vertically or diagonally. In **Something on the Ball**, an abstract work by American artist Stuart Davis (left), the curved lines of the lettering contrast with bold straight lines. The varying thicknesses of the lines give added contrast.

Shape
Shape is the outline or contour of a form. All shapes are related to triangles, rectangles or circles. In **Abstraction with Palette** by Arshile Gorky (below), the pink circular palette, suggested at the center of the canvas, is used to contrast with the implied red triangular shape and the black rectangles.

Value
The term value refers to the darkness or lightness of a color; it is clearly demonstrated in the gradation occurring from black to middle gray to white on the value scale shown in the Craftnotes, page 1339. The accompanying chroma scale in those Craftnotes shows what happens to the tone of a color as it is tinted (lightened) or shaded (darkened). Variations in value appear in **City of Towers** by Paul Klee (above), where black, medium and light rectangles and triangles establish the pattern.

Color
Color often sets the dominant tone of a painting. It may be used for bold contrast, as in the Gorky painting. Or one primary color may be used throughout a painting, as in this still life, **Apples and Pear** by Gustave Courbet (above), where tones of red dominate the canvas.

Texture

The texture of objects pictured on a canvas can be represented in a variety of ways. The texture of the paint itself can be altered by using additives—paint thinned with turpentine or oil becomes more transparent, for example. How the paint is applied will also affect its texture. Heavy brush strokes create a rough surface, smooth strokes a glossy one. The visual impression of texture is essentially the result of contrasts between dark and light areas, as in **Still Life** by Karl Knaths (right).

Composition

To work as a unit, the various elements of the painting must be put together in such a way as to move the eye over the canvas. This requires repetition of elements with variations. In **Three Musicians** by Pablo Picasso (above), the color black, used for one musician, is repeated in the black rectangles that frame the group. The eye is moved from one black rectangle to the next. Similarly, gray and red, repeated at different points on the canvas, cause a movement of the eye. Together the colors and patterns provide contrast and still unify the work.

Space

Space in a painting is established by the position, size and color of the shapes used, creating a sense of relative closeness or distance. The painting **Landscape** by George Inness (above) vividly demonstrates this three-dimensional illusion. Near objects, such as the tree at the far right, are larger in scale, more detailed, and darker in color than those in the distance, such as the bushes lining the horizon.

Materials available for an artist's use are many and varied, including paints, canvas or other painting surfaces, brushes, turpentine, palette and palette knives. Yet an adequate beginner's studio can be set up quite inexpensively. Oil (or acrylic) paints can be intermixed so that a very few colors will produce a limitless rainbow. Inexpensive painting surfaces—bond paper, wrapping paper, hardboard and the like—can be substituted for canvas. Or the artist can stretch and prepare his own canvas at great savings.

Materials

In addition to a surface to paint on, you will need a large palette (24 by 28 inches) for holding and mixing the paint, as pictured above. Any nonabsorbent surface will do—a sheet of glass, metal or plastic, or even a piece of shellacked cardboard. Brushes should range from ½ inch to 2 inches wide and should include both flat and round types. Either sable or sabeline (imitation sable) brushes may be used, but in either case, the brushes should have long hair and long handles. Flat brushes are held at the end of the handle to make broad, flowing strokes, as when backgrounds are filled in. Round-tipped brushes are held nearer the tip when fine details are added. At least one 4-inch-wide nylon or bristle brush is needed for filling in backgrounds and priming the canvas.

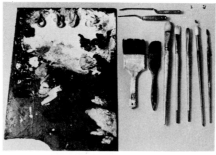

In addition, you will need a tapered palette knife with a raised handle for mixing paint on the palette and for scraping the palette clean. A selection of brushes and palette knives and a hardboard palette are shown in the photograph at the top of this column. Paints should include primary colors, secondary colors, black, white, and the so-called earth tones as shown on the opposite page.

In addition, you will need turpentine and stand oil for thinning paint and cleaning brushes; containers with metal lids to hold these solvents; jars for cleaning brushes; and plenty of rags and newspapers. (Note: since these materials are flammable, keep the containers closed when they are not in use. Work in a ventilated room, and dispose of all rags saturated with turpentine in a safe manner.)

Also convenient are a smock or apron and a paint box at least 12 by 16 inches in which to cart materials. Easels allow you to move freely and to view a canvas from various angles. A standing or folding aluminum easel that tilts can be found at any art supply store. Finally, you will need drawing supplies—a ruler, charcoal sticks, ebony pencils, pastels, and a 9-by-12-inch sketch pad.

Maintenance

Painting tools will last for a long time if they are cared for properly. Brushes should be cleaned immediately after use with turpentine, then washed in lukewarm water. (Avoid hot water—it dissolves the glue binding the brush and harms the natural bristles.) When you are not using the brushes, store them—bristles up—in a tall container; otherwise the brush will lose its shape. Scrape the palette clean at frequent intervals; the paint will stay usable for at least a week.

Stretching Canvas

Art suppliers sell stretched canvas that is already primed. But if you prefer, you can prepare your own. To do so, you will need four stretcher strips, the lengths determined by the size canvas you want to paint. You will also need a roll of cotton canvas; metal square; craft knife; staple gun; canvas pliers; acrylic gesso; and a 4-inch-wide brush.

To stretch the canvas, fit the stretchers together by interlocking the corners. Use a square to make sure the corners form right angles; then staple the joints (top photograph, below). Cut a piece of canvas 4 inches longer and wider than the outside dimensions of the stretcher frame. Stretch this over the edges and staple it to the back of the frame at the middle of one of the four sides. Pull the canvas taut with the canvas pliers, and tack it to the center of the opposite side (middle photograph, below). Staple the center of the remaining two sides in the same way. Alternating sides, pull the canvas taut with the pliers, and staple along the back of the frame at 3-inch intervals (bottom photograph, below).

THE ARTIST'S STUDIO

Priming the Canvas

Canvas must be prepared for oil painting, or it will absorb paint, deteriorating the canvas. To prepare the canvas, give it a coat or two of acrylic gesso, letting it dry between coats. To prepare the frame from warping, let the canvas lie flat while the gesso dries.

The charts (bottom right) illustrate the change in value that occurs as white becomes gray and then black.

Above left:
Cadmium yellow light
Phtalocyanine blue
Alizarin crimson

Above right:
Cadmium yellow medium
Ultramarine blue
Cadmium red light

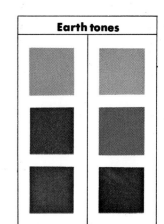

Above left:
Yellow ochre
Raw sienna
Raw umber

Above right:
Indian red
Burnt sienna
Burnt umber

Color wheel

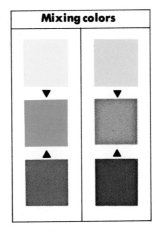

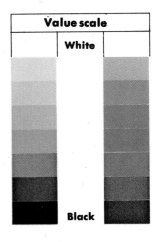

Mixing Paints

As shown on the color wheel above, red, blue and yellow are the primary colors in painting. Any of the three pure secondary colors can be made by mixing the two appropriate primaries. Red and blue yield purple, red and yellow yield orange, blue and yellow yield green. But the use of prepared secondary colors will eliminate the mixing chore.

The colors on your palette can be limited to the three primaries, the three secondaries, black, white and a selection of earth tones, but it is advisable to have a pair of each of the primaries—a cool and a warm hue of each (top center). Coolness and warmth of color refer to properties that the color will have on the canvas. A warm color will seem to come forward, a cool color will seem to recede. The coolness or warmth of a color also affects the color mixed from it. A cool yellow and a cool blue will produce a bright green, but a warm yellow and a warm blue will produce an olive green (bottom center). A moderate selection of earth tones (top right) will let you give tones and shadows to your painting.

To lighten colors so you can achieve tints, gradually add titanium white. The darker values of a color are called shades. A warm hue can be darkened by mixing it with the same color in a cooler hue. Or the three primary colors—red, yellow and blue—can be mixed to get a very dark gray for darkening colors; if the amount of yellow is decreased, the color becomes almost black. Gray tones used to darken colors can also be made by mixing complementary colors, blue with orange, red with green, or yellow with purple.

Thinning Paint

To thin paint, you need turpentine and stand oil or linseed oil. Different qualities are needed in the paints at different stages of the painting. Mixing calls for patience and practice. In the early stages of a work, you will want thin paint that will dry quickly. You might use a mixture of nine parts turpentine to one part of stand oil—added as needed to thin the oil paint. For richer color as the painting progresses, decrease the amount of turpentine until you are working with a ratio of perhaps four parts turpentine to one part stand oil. This mixture takes longer to dry, however, and you must allow each coat to dry long enough to avoid blending paint and muddying the colors.

2: With his eyes fixed on his mirror image, not on the paper, the artist made this contour drawing. He recorded the surface edge of his features and surroundings with a pen. The part-by-part approach forced him to recognize details by focusing his eyes on each part of the mirrored model.

3: To make this gesture drawing, the artist first indicated the broadest visual aspects of his anatomy as reflected in the mirror. Then he worked toward detailing more specific proportions, establishing the circular head, the triangular nose, the rectangular shoulders and so forth.

The Quick Sketch

There are two major methods of making the rough preliminary sketch that helps you establish your composition before you paint. One is contour drawing, the part-by-part approach, and the other is gesture drawing, known as the whole approach. Either can be done with pencils, ink or charcoal on a sketch pad.

To make a contour drawing, you work directly from a living model or inanimate object. Fix your eye on an edge of the shape you intend to draw. Then, either without looking at your sketch pad or looking alternately at your pad and the model, trace the outline you are looking at as though your pencil were touching that edge (photograph 2). This contour method develops your sensitivity to detail, and it may demonstrate to you the role that accident can play in the creative process. When you fix your eye on a part rather than a whole, the relationship of that part to others may become distorted, and this often creates a more spontaneous line, shape or expression than would otherwise evolve.

Gesture drawing was used in the portrait in photograph 3. Here, the artist used charcoal to rough in the broad planes and masses of the face and figure, capturing the largest visual contrasts first—the circle of the head and the bulk of the body. Then major divisions like the triangles of the nose, cheek and chin were blocked in with a concern for proportion and relative position. Only then were details clarified part by part, first with light "gestural" lines that could easily be changed. When these seemed right, the artist developed the light and shaded areas. In the example shown, one eye is defined more clearly than the other to show that a gesture drawing can be just as realistic and detailed as you wish.

Appearances Are Deceptive

If one trick of an artist is being able to see things as they usually aren't (as in the collage, page 1334), another equally vital trick is being able to record precisely what is seen—not what the artist thinks he sees or remembers to be true. Knowing how to create an illusion of depth on a flat surface is useful in any painting—even the most abstract.

There are two types of perspective that can be used to create the illusion of a three-dimensional world on a two-dimensional canvas: atmospheric perspective and linear perspective. The first, atmospheric perspective, refers to the fact that every object or scene gets grayer in its far parts. This is due to the veil formed by the atmosphere, which gets denser with increasing distance. As shown in the cityscape on page 1345, buildings or trees that might appear in strong, definite colors in the foreground of a canvas seem to be gray masses at a distance in the background of the painting.

Linear perspective stems from the fact that objects of the same size appear to grow smaller and less detailed with increasing distance. They may also appear to

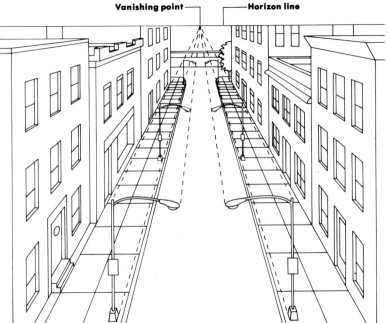

A

Figure A: In one-point perspective, the viewer's eyes are presumed to be focused on one point on the horizon, an arbitrary horizontal line on the canvas. This focus—the vanishing point—is the point where all perspective lines would converge if extended. The front tops and bottoms of objects are parallel to the horizon line; the front side edges are perpendicular to it. The effect of depth is conveyed by angled side lines that converge on the vanishing point and by the use of shorter vertical lines to represent the far end of each object rather than the near end.

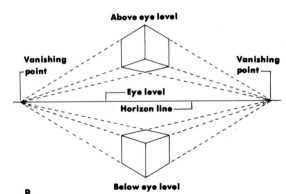

B

Figure B: In two-point perspective, the viewer's eyes are presumed to be focused on the near edge of an object in the composition. Vanishing lines are drawn from this edge to two points on the horizon line since adjacent sides of the object will be disappearing from view at two angles. As in one-point perspective, all vertical lines representing the edges of objects are drawn perpendicular to the horizon line, but tops and bottoms of objects are represented by angled lines parallel to the imaginary lines to the vanishing points.

recede into the distance at an angle (Figures A and B). What the angle is will depend on the presumed view point. Two types of perspective are emphasized in the projects here. The cityscape, page 1345, suggests a one-point perspective, where the eyes of artist and viewer are focused on one point on the horizon at the upper right and all lines converge at that point. This is called a vanishing point because as the objects represented get smaller and smaller, they eventually vanish on the eye-level horizon.

In the still life on page 1343 some of the objects on the table were sketched in two-point perspective, similar to that in Figure B. In two-point perspective, the eyes focus on an object in such a way that imaginary perspective lines could be drawn to two vanishing points on the horizon, rather than only one. In actual appearance, objects diminish upward and downward as well as to the sides if they are viewed from above or below the eye-level horizon.

Lightly penciled converging lines that meet at vanishing points, plus a horizon line, can be of great help in understanding and establishing perspective.

Direct painting: the still life

This photograph shows fabrics and objects as they were arranged by the artist before he began painting the still life on the opposite page.

The success of any painting depends first on its composition—how the elements work together to form a single whole. The following guidelines will help you get started. Choose objects that establish a dominant shape with repetition, but let them contrast in size, texture and color. This dominant shape, which may be the largest and the most repeated shape in the painting, should be emphasized by secondary contrasting shapes. In the still life shown at left, for example, the angular bust is emphasized by the slender wine bottle and the short, round pots on the table. Colors should be repeated throughout a canvas to establish an overall color scheme. The repetition of like colors (with some variation in hue) helps move the viewer's eye from one point to another, and this is a vital part of composition. In the still life shown on the opposite page, shades of blue and green are dominant, and color helps unify the composition, moving the viewer's eye from the drapery across the canvas to the table coverings. Even the white plaster bust has blue and green shadows in it, adding unity to the painting. The background color and texture should be a foil for the main subject matter, complementing it but not competing with it. Finally, the center of interest should not be at the physical center of the canvas. In the still life, for example, the bust and bottle are placed to the left of the canvas center.

The still life is one of the best subjects for learning composition. Lighting can be kept constant over a long period of time, and objects of the composition are easily found—in the attic, on nature walks or even in the refrigerator. (Many a bowl of fruit has been food for the artist as well as for his composition.)

Keeping these principles in mind, try setting up various still life compositions and seeing which ones work best. Once the composition is arranged, view it from different angles to find which is most effective. The still life shown could have been painted head on, for example, but it worked better when viewed from above. Rather than having a hard edge of the table forming a horizontal line through the middle of the canvas, the table coverings formed interesting triangular and rectangular color divisions, and the table itself became a circular shape to echo the pots.

The still life was done with a process known as direct painting. By this method, the color desired is mixed on the palette and then put on the canvas to create an image as directly and immediately as possible. If the effect is pleasing, this

To start his still life painting, the artist freely sketched a contour drawing with charcoal. Then he began to establish color relationships and the highlights and shadows on each object in the composition. By painting with actual colors in this very general way, he formed an overall pattern of light and dark.

At this point, the whole canvas was covered with little but color relationships. By working quickly in different areas of the canvas, the artist was able to develop in a short time, a total color relationship that he could judge. This helped him to achieve a balance of color throughout the canvas.

becomes the painting. If it is not, the artist must mix again and try again, perhaps many times, until he is satisfied with the result.

Express Yourself

To begin the still life, the artist coated the canvas with thin raw sienna to establish an even background color; then he made a preliminary sketch on the canvas with charcoal (lower left, opposite page) indicating the major shapes and proportions without getting involved with details.

It is helpful at this point to think less of what is represented in the still life than of the composition itself—the position of shapes, line, color, values, space and textural contrast. In this still life, the draperies could have become colored rectangles, the tablecloth might have evolved into a green circle, the table covering into a blue triangle, the bottle and bust could have been represented as a white cylinder and oval, the pots as red and green circles. And it is entirely possible that such an abstraction might have been more successful as a painting than the representational one shown. Through experimentation you can develop your own style.

The charcoal sketch that originally outlined the objects in this still life was deliberately left exposed through these stages to clarify the method of direct painting that was used. This painting is now near completion. The artist may choose to leave some areas flat while he adds modeling shadows to others to create depths and movement.

Once the charcoal sketch was made, the next step was to mix paint to establish the basic colors quickly, and to establish the color values needed (lower right, opposite page). (This is often a confusing concept. The value is the overall lightness or darkness created by the effect of light on color. For example, red as in the pot on the table is always red, but where the pot is in shadow (left hand edge), the value is darker.) Working within the charcoal lines, the artist established the colors, then the main differences between shadow and light by painting in tints and shades of the color originally blocked in. Other colors added to the effect of modeling—green and purple were used to fill in shadows and highlights of the blue curtains.

Once the blocked-in colors were dry, the artist could paint details in any area until he was satisfied with the result. Varying the brush strokes from area to area helped create texture and add interest to the painting. By switching occasionally from one part of the canvas to another, the artist kept all areas related.

Paint and Color
Indirect painting: the cityscape $ 🖼 👤 🎨

Indirect painting, in contrast to the direct painting done in the still life, is painting by building up an image with many layers of paint. These layers, successively applied, modify one another so no part of the painting is complete until the last strokes are applied. A scene such as the cityscape, consisting of broad, flat areas, lends itself well to this kind of painting.

To begin the cityscape, the artist covered the canvas with a thin coat of raw sienna paint. When the canvas was thoroughly dry, he used a 4-inch-wide flat nylon brush to indicate the broadest areas for color (below, left). This is a different approach from the one used in the still life (page 1342) that started with the outline of a charcoal sketch; however, either method can be used to begin a painting. Since the majority of shapes in the cityscape are linear and tend to overlap as they go back in perspective, the artist decided to forego a preliminary sketch. He applied broad masses of color first — a phthalocyanine blue rectangle to indicate the receding street in the left foreground, and a thinned ultramarine blue square on top of that to locate the flat plane of the storefront at left of center. Two vertical lines, one light and the other dark, suggest two figures; horizontal lines stand for street corners and the horizon; a pale blue shape suggests the shadow cast by the buildings; yellow ochre represents the street and distant buildings; a soft, blue tint will become the sky (below, right).

Once these major areas were blocked in, they could be modified and defined. To do this, the artist mixed small amounts of paint on the palette with a palette knife and his brush. By varying the mixture a bit at a time, he could create many different tints and shades, avoiding a flat mass of only one color. For the initial layers, he mixed enough turpentine with the oil paint to get a thin, fast-drying, relatively transparent color. This allowed colors to be built up gradually, giving substance to the image. As the final layers neared, the amount of turpentine was

To start the cityscape shown on the opposite page, the artist first used these broad brush strokes to establish mass relationships. In this way, he was able to define a pattern of dark and light areas.

He began to modify the massive shapes of the cityscape in a general way. This determined the location of the climax area at center left. Here the canvas is filled with structural contrasts—the dark, rectangular buildings, the light triangular street, and the repetitions of vertical movement. The street scene is dominated by blue, yellows in opposition, and pink and red are minor color notes.

decreased to provide richer color. The artist's first concern was with the most obvious contrasts—the white vertical lamp posts against the dark rectangular building, the white carriage blanket against the dark figure, the horizontal signs on the buildings, the vertical windows, and the shading of the buildings in the distance in relationship to those in the foreground.

Paint was applied in a series of stages, gradually moving the composition from general masses toward defined, finished images. To summarize these stages, the artist first applied thinned color with a large brush to establish general shape ideas. Then he used definite colors applied with smaller brush strokes to focus in on these nebulous shapes. In the last stage, details were added so that these abstractions could represent people, cars, buildings and other objects in the cityscape. (It is essential in this type of painting to avoid blending strokes. Paint is applied only as long as clean, definite brush strokes can be applied; then the artist must let the paint dry to avoid muddy colors.) Smaller and smaller brush strokes were used until the artist was satisfied with the details (below). Notice how the figures, street and storefront in the foreground are more clearly defined in color and shape than those in the distance nearer to the horizon line.

The artist continued to adjust and define the visual and structural relationships until they reached the image that he had in mind. Another artist might view this work as finished in the first stage, or he might continue working until he added much more detail.

Underpainting: the portrait $ 🎨 👤 🎨

The artist first coated the canvas with sienna thinned with turpentine (above). Over this background, he applied unthinned white paint to establish the overall highlights. More raw umber paint was used to establish the darkest areas. To ensure color brilliance in later stages, a thin coat of white was applied to the entire canvas. Over the original layer of sienna and white, colors were applied (above). Often much of the color was wiped away before it dried (scumbled) to preserve a luminous quality. Unthinned white was applied lightly at each stage.

There is one specialized form of indirect painting—called underpainting—that stems from the Renaissance procedure of separating the drawing process from the coloring process. With this technique, the painting starts with highlights (in white) and dark areas (in earth tones) applied on a neutral background. Then many thin, semi-transparent layers of color are applied. If the effect is right and the color is left in place, it is called a glaze; more often, it is partly wiped away, a process called scumbling. The highlights and shadows are reinforced as the painting progresses.

Although this process can take months to complete, the effect gained is a deep richness with lustrous color.

The portrait opposite is an example of underpainting. Here, the artist started with a series of loose gesture drawings (page 1340) to establish the basic masses and the composition, then did a full-size (18 by 24 inches) charcoal sketch. When he was satisfied with the effect, he began the actual painting by coating the prepared canvas with a layer of thin umber paint. (In spite of the many coats of paint added later, some of this background shows through in the final painting as modeling shadows.) Using charcoal, the artist copied his final sketch onto this ground.

The next step called for what is termed a dry-brush technique. Unthinned white paint, just as it comes from the tube, was brushed onto the canvas to establish the various light areas of the image (top left, above). By varying the pressure on the brush, the artist could vary the effect achieved—from a solid white, opaque line or plane to the lightest of transparent touches. Similarly, the dark areas of the hair were strengthened with raw umber. But most of the shadows are the background color showing through. Once this first coat was dry, the artist used a dry brush barely touching the canvas to go over the entire painting with white, so succeeding colors would be more lustrous.

It is essential with the underpainting technique that each layer be allowed to dry; otherwise colors will become muddy. It is a good idea to work for several hours; then abandon the painting for several days. When you return, the paint will be dry and your vision will be refreshed.

Once the artist was satisfied with the highlights and shadows he had established he began to put on thin layers of color, initially thinned with a mixture of 9 parts turpentine to 1 part stand oil (top right, opposite page). This produced a thin wash, desirably translucent and fast drying. Wiping away most of the first layers with a rag (scumbling) served to keep the colors from obscuring the highlights and shadows; to preserve or elaborate detail, more white or earth tone was added. And after each stage, a very thin layer of white was dry-brushed over the painting to give brilliance to the color and a luminous quality to the image. With the repeated wiping and glazing, it is possible to achieve almost infinite color variations.

Painting textures such as hair or cloth requires careful observation of the play of light and shadow. Hair is soft and silky; it was depicted here with a flat bristle brush and unthinned paint, with special attention to loose strands of hair around the temples, ears and neck. Soft materials, such as the green wool dress, have fuzzy outlines; hard-edged objects have sharp outlines. The white collar of the dress is lightly shaded with gray. Background colors were chosen to give a feeling of spaciousness and to set off the figure without being distracting.

Scumbling (wiping away) and glazing (using very thin paint) keep each layer of color semi-transparent. The portrait is dominated by a diamond shape; the circular shape of the head opposes the rectangular shape of the canvas. Yellow-green and gray-green are the main colors; the reds are in opposition.

OJO DE DIOS
Winding Luck

The *ojo de dios*, literally translated from the Spanish as "eye of god," is a symbol of the power of seeing and understanding unknown things. Although the *ojo* is most commonly found among the Huichol Indians of northwestern Mexico, it has been observed as far south as Peru and as far east as Egypt. East or west, the design is always the same: two crossed sticks wrapped from the center outward with colorful yarns to form a diamond pattern. The centermost part, or the pupil of the eye, is usually wrapped in such a way that a smooth, flat surface is created, leaving the sticks exposed on the back. There are many variations for wrapping the yarn around the outer part of the sticks—each resulting in a unique *ojo de dios*.

The Origins

The Huichol Indians are pantheistic, and the four points of the cross that forms the frame of the *ojo* represent earth, fire, air and water. In making an *ojo*, the Indian expresses a prayer that the eye of some particular spirit may rest on him. When an *ojo* is completed, it is placed in the tribal god-house or in some sacred area reserved for the god being addressed.

Since the infant mortality rate is high, one of the most fervent Huichol prayers is for the life of a newborn child. At birth, the child's grandfather or a reigning elder makes an *ojo*. Once a year, the child's hair is cut by that sponsor; the hair and a small additional eye are added to the original *ojo*, a symbolic way of asking for continued life. After the hair has been cut five times and five eyes have been added to the original, the *ojo* is complete and is left in the god-house as a continuing prayer that the child may not become critically ill.

The Huichol Indians make *ojos de dios* to ask the gods to watch over many aspects of their lives. A small eye with a crudely embroidered piece of cloth attached becomes a prayer that the child may be successful in learning to embroider. An eye with a small piece of textile attached serves as a prayer that the god may help the weaver. An eye that is wound with cotton fiber represents a prayer for a bountiful crop. One attached to a wooden stool and left in the god-house is a carpenter's prayer for skill in his work. During the ceremony of first fruits, both children and harvested vegetables are decorated with *ojos* because both are fruits of the Indians. The children are dedicated to the gods in this ceremony that symbolizes the hopes of the Huichols for their young.

Modern Adaptations

The *ojo de dios*, still symbolizing a desire for health, fortune and long life, is decorative as well. Variations on the basic design are endless; directions for making several types, including a wall hanging, a mobile and a necklace, are on pages that follow. Colors can be coordinated with those in the room where the *ojo* will be displayed, or can be dictated by the colors of leftover yarns available. Making an *ojo* for a friend is one way of wishing him good fortune in an ancient Indian tradition. The traditional *ojo* is 15 inches high, but 4-foot versions have also been made. Regardless of size, the basic windings are the same. Given large dowels and plenty of yarn, any of the following *ojos* can be made as big as you want.

Materials and Tools

To make the *ojos de dios* on the following pages, you will need four-ply knitting worsted in various colors (leftover yarn is fine), round wooden dowels and white glue. The tools include a craft knife to notch the dowels, wire to hold them while the glue dries, an ice cream stick or other applicator to spread the glue, a clothespin to hold the yarn between windings, and a small scissors to cut the yarn.

Judith Pickett, born in Montgomery, Alabama, is a graduate of Montclair (New Jersey) State College. She taught art in high school and nursery school, and ceramics at the Brick Kiln Pottery School in New York. An exhibit of her stuffed sculpture was shown at Webb and Parsons Gallery in Bedford, New York. She is presently a crafts designer for a national woman's magazine.

1: Materials needed to make an *ojo de dios* are yarn, wire, dowels, and white glue. A craft knife, ice cream stick, clothespin, and small scissors are the necessary tools.

The many angles and planes of this three-dimensional *ojo de dios* resemble the orbits and planets of a galaxy, as this mobile is appropriately called.

CRAFTNOTES: OJO CONSTRUCTION

Basic Ojo Wraps

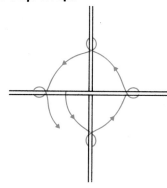

The flat wrap is the simplest wrap; it is always used to form the eye at the center of an **ojo** design. Holding the yarn securely behind the intersection of the dowels, wind it over and around each dowel in turn.

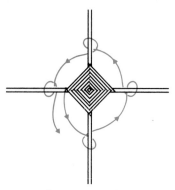

The recessed wrap gives depth to an **ojo** design; it is the reverse of the flat wrap. Holding the yarn securely, wind it under and around each dowel in turn.

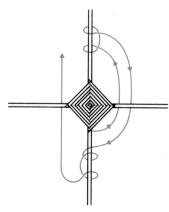

Arrowing adds another point of interest to an **ojo**. After completing the last wrap, attach the yarn, and bring it across the back of the eye to the opposite dowel. Wrap the yarn under and around the

dowel twice; then go back to the dowel where you started and wrap the yarn under and around that dowel twice. Continue until the arrow head is finished. Repeat on the other two dowel arms.

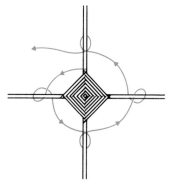

The alternating flat and recess wrap makes an **ojo** flat on two dowels and recessed on two. Take the yarn behind and around the first dowel, over and around the second one, behind and around the third, and over and around the fourth.

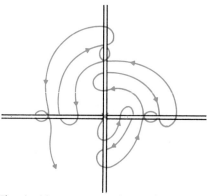

The double wrap is used to make an **ojo** flat on both sides of the dowel frame. After tying the yarn to the dowel intersection, bring the yarn over and across two adjacent dowels twice, then under and around the second of the two dowels once. Repeat around all dowels in turn.

Pompons

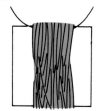

To make a pompon, cut a piece of cardboard 3 to 4 inches wide. Put a 6-inch piece of yarn across the top of the cardboard for the tie, holding it with a long piece of yarn wound 25 to 50 times around the cardboard.

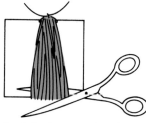

Knot the ends of the tie, securing the strands of yarn, and cut the loops at the opposite side of the cardboard. Repeat for as many pompons as there are dowel ends.

To attach a pompon to a dowel end, apply glue to the knot and the dowel end. Place the knot on the tip of the dowel with the yarn ends pointing toward the center of the eye.

With a 6-inch piece of yarn, tie the pompon to the dowel about ½ inch from the end.

Flip the yarn ends in the opposite direction so they point outward, and tie again with another piece of yarn. Trim the ends and fluff the pompon. Repeat for each dowel end.

The color scheme for this *ojo de dios* was chosen from leftover yarn specifically to coordinate with the room in which it hangs.

Weaving, Braiding, Knotting
Flat ojo de dios

¢ ☒ 👫 🔥

To make the flat *ojo de dios*, you need two ¼-inch dowels, each 14 inches long; leftover yarn in three colors; and white glue. Notch the center of each dowel with a craft knife. Put glue in these notches, cross the dowels at right angles so the notches interlock, and hold them together temporarily with wire (photograph 2). Let the glue dry for 45 minutes; then remove the wire.

2: Use wire to hold the notched dowels together temporarily while the glue between them dries.

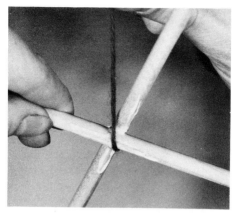

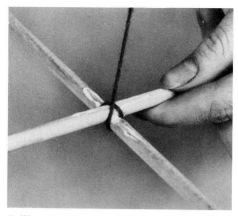

3: Run a line of glue along the joined dowels before wrapping to keep the yarn from slipping.

4: Hold the yarn behind one dowel and bring it diagonally across the front of the intersection.

5: Wrap the yarn around the dowels and back across the intersection on the opposite diagonal.

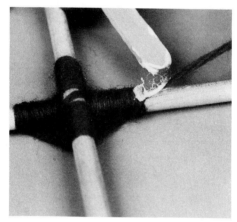

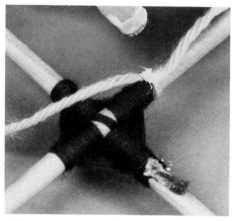

6: To complete one yarn color, make a single knot on the back of the last dowel wrapped.

7: Cut off any excess yarn, and glue a 1-inch tail to the back of a dowel.

8: Knot and glue a new color yarn on the back of the next dowel in succession.

To keep the yarn from slipping, run a line of glue for an inch or so along the back of both dowels at the intersection (photograph 3). With the first color of yarn, hold an end in back of a dowel and bring the yarn forward diagonally across the intersection (photograph 4), under one dowel arm and back across the intersection on the opposite diagonal (photograph 5). Using a flat wrap (Craftnotes, page 1350), wind an eye that measures 1 inch across. Stretch the yarn slightly as you wind, keeping an even tension so the yarn won't sag. Make a single knot around the last dowel (photograph 6); clip the yarn, leaving a 1-inch tail to glue to the dowel (photograph 7). To change colors, attach yarn of the new color to the dowel next in succession to the one where you ended the first color. Knot the yarn around the dowel, again leaving a tail to be glued to the dowel (photograph 8). Put a line of glue on the back of the dowels and continue flat-wrapping with the second color (photograph 9) until the eye measures 2½ inches across. Change to the third color, following the same procedure, and continue flat-wrapping until the eye measures 4 inches across. Always put a line of glue on the dowels before wrapping to secure the yarn. Attach the first color again, and continue flat-wrapping until the eye measures 6 inches across. Attach the second color, and switching to a recessed wrap (Craftnotes, page 1350 and photograph 10), wrap until the *ojo* measures 8 inches across.

The next step is arrowing (Craftnotes, page 1350). Knot and glue the first color of yarn to the last dowel wrapped. In arrowing, the yarn is wrapped from one dowel arm to its opposite arm (photograph 11). Continue arrowing until the *ojo* measures 9½ inches across. Repeat with the other two dowel arms. Most of the arrowing yarn lies on the back of the *ojo;* only the arrow shows from the front (photograph 12, opposite page).

To cover each exposed dowel end, put glue on the back and wrap it tightly with yarn, using the second color of yarn. Secure this wrap by knotting (photograph 13)

9: As this front view shows, wrap the new-color yarn around each dowel in succession—the same way as with yarn of the first color.

10: To make a recessed wrap as shown above, you just reverse the flat wrap, bringing the yarn under the dowel and around.

11: This back view shows how arrowing is done; two opposite dowels are wrapped. Most of the yarn is visible only from the back.

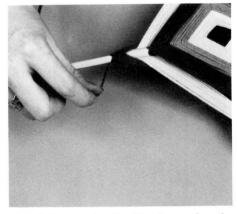

12: Only the arrowhead itself can be seen from the front on each of the dowels.

13: To finish a dowel end, wrap yarn around it until it is covered. Secure the yarn end with a knot.

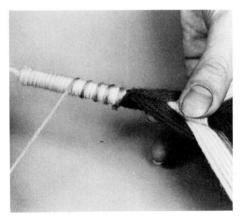

14: A second color of yarn can be wrapped on dowel ends, leaving a space between the wraps so the first color shows through.

15: To secure a pompon on a dowel, tie it in place about ½ inch from the end.

16: Flip the pompon yarn ends so they point out and tie again, ½ inch beyond the first tie.

and gluing the yarn end. For a decorative touch, go over this wrap with yarn of the third color, leaving space between the wraps so the second color shows through (photograph 14). Secure this end by knotting and gluing.

Pompons give the finishing touch. Make four using a cardboard 3 inches wide (see Craftnotes, page 1350). Put a pompon over a dowel end, and tie it so the ends of yarn point toward the center eye. Tie it about ½ inch down from the end of the dowel (photograph 15). Now flip the ends of yarn over this tie so they point away from the center eye. Tie the pompon again, about ½ inch outside the first tie (photograph 16). Do the same on each dowel. Tie two ends of the top pompon to make a loop for hanging.

The blue and green bands and the red and pink bands appear woven, but they are formed by winding both colors in the band with an alternating flat and recessed wrap.

A

Figure A: To make a woven-look eye (pictured right), wrap the first color (blue in the drawing) with an alternating flat and recessed wrap. Wrap the second color (green in the drawing) in the same way but starting with an opposite wrap. The bottom dowel has blue yarn going under and around it (recessed wrap) and the green yarn going over and around it (flat wrap).

Weaving, Braiding, Knotting
Woven ojo de dios

An *ojo* with a woven look is not hard to make. You will need two ¼-inch dowels, each 18 inches long; less than 1 ounce each of 5 colors of yarn; and white glue. The woven look is created by wrapping with two colors of yarn so they give the effect of changing color. Choose colors that will contrast to emphasize this illusion. For the *ojo* pictured above, blue and green are wound together, red and pink are wound together, and purple is used as the accent color. To begin, notch both dowels at midpoint, and glue them together at right angles. Hold with wire 45 minutes while the glue dries. Remove the wire, and tie yarn of the accent color to the dowel intersection (photographs 4 and 5, page 1352). Using a flat wrap (Craftnotes, page 1350), wind an eye that measures 1½ inches across. Knot the yarn, clip it, and glue the tail to one arm. Attach the first two colors of yarn to one dowel. Wrap one color at a time, alternating flat and recessed wrapping (Figure A). The first color goes under and around the first dowel, over and around the second, under and around the third, over and around the starting dowel. Hold the yarn with a clothespin, and begin wrapping with the second color, this time going over and around the first dowel, under and around the second, over and around the third, under and around the starting dowel. Hold the yarn with a clothespin and wrap again with the first color, using the same alternating flat and recess wrap. Continue wrapping with these two colors until the eye measures 3 inches across. Knot the yarn, clip it, and glue the tail to the dowel. Attach the second pair of yarn colors to the next dowel. Following the same procedure, wrap these colors using the alternating flat and recessed wrap until the eye measures 6 inches across. Knot the yarn, clip it, and glue the tails. Attach the first pair of colors, and with the alternating wrap, continue until the *ojo* measures 7½ inches across. Attach the second pair of colors again, and with the alternating wrap, wind until the *ojo* is 12 inches across. Then attach the accent color. Using a flat wrap, wind the yarn around the dowel three times.

Cover the dowel arms by winding the accent color around each arm (photograph 13). Using one color from the second pair, wind the top and bottom dowel arms letting the accent color show through (photograph 14). Wind the side dowel ends with the other color from the second pair. Complete the *ojo* by making pompons (Craftnotes, page 1350); make two for the top and bottom dowels from one color of the first pair and two for the side dowels from the second color of the first pair. Tie two strands of the top pompon to make a loop for hanging.

Weaving, Braiding, Knotting
Ojo de dios necklace

¢ ▣ 👫 🖾

One way to pursue good luck is to wear an *ojo* necklace. The one pictured (right) has three eyes. To make it, you will need six skeins of size 3 pearl cotton—two purple, one lavender, one red, one orange, and one flesh-color; ¾ yard of round elastic cord; 21½ inches of ¼-inch plastic tubing (or any flexible tubing with a large enough opening to accommodate the elastic cord); 5 inches of ⅛-inch plastic tubing; six ⅛-inch wood dowels, three 4 inches long and three 3½ inches long; and white glue.

Notch all the dowels at the midpoint. Glue the 3½-inch dowels to the 4-inch dowels at right angles, holding them with wire until the glue dries. Beginning with red yarn, double-wrap the three small *ojos* (see Craftnotes, page 1350). Make an eye that measures 1 inch across on each. Knot the yarn, clip and glue it to the dowel. To complete the eye, wind four rounds of orange yarn, three of flesh-color, two of lavender, and three of purple.

To make the circular neckpiece, put a thin line of glue on one side of the ¼-inch plastic tubing. Tie the purple yarn around one end of the tubing and wind around the tubing until it is covered. End with a slip knot, and glue it in place. Put the elastic cord through the tubing, and tie the ends with a small knot, thus forming a circle. When the ends of tubing are pulled apart, the elastic stretches so the necklace fits over the head.

To complete the medallion, cut the ⅛-inch plastic tubing into three 1½-inch pieces and one ½-inch piece. Arrange the three *ojos* as shown (right) with the 4-inch dowels horizontal and the 3½-inch dowels vertical. Slip one 1½-inch tube onto the bottom dowel arms of each of the two end *ojos*. Bend the tubes, and slip the other end onto the horizontal arms of the center *ojo*. Slip one 1½-inch tube on the inner side arms of the end *ojos*, and the ½-inch tube on the top arm of the center *ojo*. Cut a small hole in the horizontal tubing, and put glue on the ½-inch tube and push it into the hole. Wrap all plastic tubing with purple yarn. Clip and glue all yarn ends except on the far right, far left, and bottom dowel arms. Leave a 3-inch length of purple yarn at these points where pompons will be added. Let the glue dry. Make three orange and red pompons, using a piece of cardboard 1½ inches wide (see Craftnotes, page 1350). Using the purple yarn, tie the pompons in place.

To attach the *ojo* medallion to the neckpiece, measure 2 inches on either side of the center of the neck tubing and mark these points. Moving the purple yarn aside slightly, cut small holes in the tubing at these points with the craft knife. Make the holes smaller than the ⅛-inch diameter of the dowel ends. Put glue on the dowel ends, and push them into the holes. Wrap purple yarn around these intersections to hide the joints and to help hold them together. Spread glue on the back, and let it dry before wearing.

A smile of good fortune comes easily to the wearer of an Indian *ojo* necklace, as a good luck symbol.

The snowflake *ojo de dios* is given a holiday flavor when wrapped with red and green yarn; alternatively, it could be wrapped in white yarn to resemble its outdoor counterpart.

Weaving, Braiding, Knotting
Snowflake ojo

The snowflake *ojo* looks festive when made with red and green yarn, as shown above. You will need nine ½-inch dowels, six of them 6 inches long and three 18 inches long; 1 ounce each of four-ply knitting worsted in kelly green, light green, red, maroon, and flesh-color; white glue; and a red felt-tipped marker.

Notch the midpoints of the 18-inch dowels, and glue them together at 60-degree angles; wire and let dry. Make a notch 3 inches from the end of each arm; then notch the midpoints of the six 6-inch dowels and set them aside. Remove the wire, and wrap maroon yarn around the intersection several times. Using a flat wrap (see Craftnotes, page 1350), and going around each of the six arms, make an eye that measures 2 inches across. Knot, clip, and glue the yarn. Continuing with a flat wrap, wind three rounds of red yarn. Follow this with nine rounds of flesh-colored yarn, using a recessed wrap (Craftnotes, page 1350). Attach the light green yarn, and flat wrap until the eye is 5¼ inches across. Attach the red yarn, and make one flat-wrap round. Attach the kelly green, and with a recessed wrap, wind eight rounds. Continuing with kelly green, flat wrap until the *ojo* is 7 inches wide. Attach the maroon yarn and flat wrap one round. This completes the center eye.

Matching notches made earlier, attach the six small dowels to the dowel arms at right angles. Glue and wire together, let dry, and remove wire. The six small *ojos* that surround the center eye are identical and are all made with the flat wrap. Starting with red yarn, make an eye measuring 1¼ inches across. Then wrap three rounds of maroon. Attach flesh-color yarn and wrap eight rounds. Follow with two rounds of light green, five of kelly green, and end with one round of maroon.

Using red yarn, cover all exposed dowels between the center eye and each of the six small eyes. Also with red, cover the exposed dowel ends on each of the six small *ojos*. Make six pompons (Craftnotes, page 1350) of kelly green yarn, using a 2½-inch piece of cardboard. Attach these to the ends of the six dowel arms. Using the red marker, color the ends of the six 6-inch dowels. Tie two strands of one pompon together to make a loop for hanging.

Rainbow colors are given a new dimension — a third dimension of depth, actually — in this eight-sided evening star *ojo de dios*.

Weaving, Braiding, Knotting
Evening star ojo

A suspended three-dimensional *ojo* makes an interesting mobile. The design pictured above, made of three dowels of the same length, is called evening star, an appropriate name. To make it, you will need three ½-inch dowels, each 36 inches long; one ounce each of four-ply knitting worsted in purple, blue, green, yellow, orange, and red—the main colors; less than one ounce each of four-ply knitting worsted in mauve, lavender, light blue, turquoise, light green, pale yellow, flesh-color, and pink—the accent colors; two ounces of orange rug yarn for the pompons; and white household glue. In addition to the tools listed on page 1348, you will need a drill, a small saw and a 1½-inch finishing nail.

To make the frame, notch two dowels at their midpoints. Glue and wire; let dry for 45 minutes. Saw the third dowel in half. Remove the wire from the first two dowels and, using a 1/16-inch bit, carefully drill a hole through the point where the two dowels intersect, at right angles to them. Put the nail through the hole so that each end extends ½ inch; it may help to clip the head off the finishing nail with pliers. Put glue around the nail to hold it. With the same bit, drill a hole ½ inch deep in one end of each short dowel. Fit these dowels on the nail ends and glue them in place, holding them with wire until the glue dries.

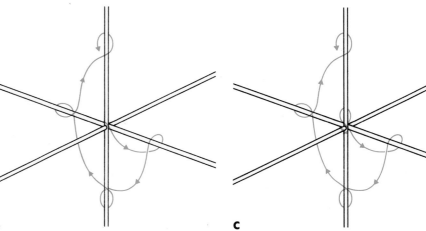

B

Figure B: To make a three-dimensional *ojo*, hold the frame so you are facing two dowels that are vertical and horizontal. Ignore, for the moment, the third dowel. Using a flat wrap, wind the yarn around the right, bottom, left, and top dowels as illustrated.

C

Figure C: When you have completed the sequence in Figure B, turn the frame one quarter-turn to the right so the third dowel is now the horizontal dowel. Again, using the flat wrap, wind the yarn around what are now the right, bottom, left, and top dowels.

Since this *ojo* will be viewed from all sides, each side is wrapped identically. A flat wrap (see Craftnotes, page 1350) is used, but it is worked three-dimensionally in this way: hold the frame so one dowel is vertical and one horizontal. Tie the yarn to the top dowel, and put glue on an inch or two of each dowel. Starting from the top dowel, bring the yarn over and around the right, bottom, and left dowels and then back over and around the top dowel on which you started (Figure B). Still holding the bottom dowel, turn the frame one quarter turn to the right so the dowel that was pointing at you is now the right dowel. Repeat the wrap with what are now the right, bottom, left, and top dowels (Figure C). Continue wrapping, rotating the frame one quarter-turn to the right after each round. Use a clothespin to hold the yarn in place when one color is finished, and you are ready to knot and glue the end to a dowel. Before you end a color, make sure you have wrapped an equal number of rounds on all sides. The color sequence is as follows: start with red yarn and wrap until the radius of the eye (measuring from the intersection out) is 1¼ inches. Follow with five rounds of pink, four of flesh-color, a 1-inch band of orange (1 inch equals approximately 15 rounds), three rounds of flesh-color, four of pale yellow, a 1-inch band of yellow, five rounds of pale yellow, three of light green, a 1-inch band of green, three rounds of light green, four of turquoise, a 1¼-inch band of blue, six rounds of light blue, five of lavender, a 1-inch band of purple, and end with four rounds of mauve. With the wrapping finished, the eye should have a radius of 9½ inches in all directions from the center.

To finish the dowel ends, put glue on each dowel, and wrap it with red yarn. Using a 4-inch piece of cardboard, make six pompons of orange rug yarn, and attach them to the dowel ends (see Craftnotes, page 1350). Tie two strands of the top pompon to make a loop, and hang the evening star in a place where it is free to move, thus exposing all eight sides.

The pompons are planets, the path of the yarn is the orbit, the center eye is the sun, and this *ojo* mobile is our galaxy viewed from outer space.

Weaving, Braiding, Knotting
Galaxy

The spectacular three-dimensional *ojo* pictured at left is called the galaxy. It is most impressive when it is hung in a space where light can play on its many angles and planes. (Another view of the galaxy appears on page 1349). To make the galaxy, you will need four ½-inch dowels—one 36 inches long, one 18 inches, and two 12 inches; the tools listed on page 1348, and approximately eight ounces of yarn in a variety of weights and colors. The beauty of this *ojo* stems from the fact that yarn weights can range from the traditional four-ply knitting worsted to heavy-weight yarn, sport yarn, baby yarn, even hand-spun yarn. Any and all leftover yarn can be used; each combination will create a unique *ojo*.

To make the frame, notch the 36-inch dowel 9 inches in from either end. Notch the midpoint of each 12-inch dowel. Join them to the 36-inch dowel so they are parallel to each other. Glue and wire them together. Notch the midpoint of both the 36-inch dowel and the 18-inch dowel. Join them so the 18-inch dowel is at right angles to the two 12-inch dowels (Figure D). Glue and wire together. Let dry for at least 45 minutes; then remove the wires.

Begin by making three eyes on the 36-inch dowel at the intersections with the three smaller dowels. The center eye will be at right angles to the top and bottom eyes. Use a double wrap (see Craftnotes, page 1350) so the eye is flat on both sides. Make each eye 1¾ inches wide. Knot and glue the yarn. Run a line of glue along the 36-inch dowel between the eyes and wrap the dowel with the same color of yarn; then knot and glue the ends.

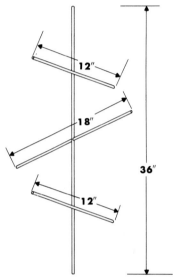

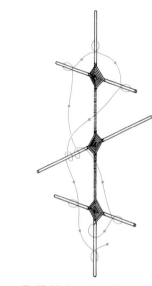

D

Figure D: For the galaxy frame, put a 12-inch dowel 9 inches in from each end of a 36-inch dowel, keeping them parallel to each other. Position an 18-inch dowel midway between the 12-inch dowels and at right angles to them.

E

Figure E: Hold the galaxy frame so you are facing the two 12-inch dowels and the middle 18-inch dowel is pointing at you. Wrap the yarn, starting under the "eye of god" on the bottom dowel following the path indicated above.

F

Figure F: Turn the frame so you are facing the other side of the two 12-inch dowels and the opposite end of the 18-inch dowel is pointing at you; then wrap the yarn, following the path indicated in the drawing above.

To start the three-dimensional wrapping, tie a new color yarn to the vertical dowel at the base of the bottom eye. Hold the bottom of the 36-inch dowel in one hand and wrap the yarn with the other hand. With the 18-inch dowel facing you, bring the yarn across the bottom dowel, over and around the bottom right dowel, over and around the middle dowel, over and around the top left dowel, over and around the top dowel, over and around the top right dowel. Bring the yarn down to the middle dowel, go under and around it, then over and around the bottom left dowel, and over and around the bottom dowel (Figure E). Holding the yarn securely, turn the frame so the opposite side of the 18-inch dowel faces you. Bring the yarn over and around the bottom right dowel, over and around the middle dowel, over and around the top left dowel, over and around the top dowel, over and around the top right dowel, under and around the middle dowel, over and around the bottom left dowel, and over and around the bottom dowel (Figure F). Repeat these steps until the color band is as wide as you want. Before changing colors, make sure that you have wrapped both sides the same number of times. End and start all new colors at the bottom dowel. Continue wrapping until the yarn from the center eye out to any dowel measures about 4 inches. This will leave about 1 inch of exposed dowel on either end of the 12-inch dowels.

To finish the *ojo*, run a line of glue on all exposed dowel ends, and cover with the same color yarn used for the eyes. Using a 3-inch piece of cardboard, make eight pompons in the same main color, and attach them to the dowel ends (see Craftnotes, page 1350). Tie two strands from the top pompon to make a loop for hanging.

For related crafts and projects, see the entries "Mobiles" and "Yarn Painting."

ORGANIC GARDENING
Harvesting the Good Earth

In gardening, the term *organic* refers to a way of growing plants naturally, without the help of synthetic fertilizers or toxic pesticides. The key word is "naturally," not "organic." Organic gardeners do use a lot of organic materials (those derived from living organisms) in their soil conditioners, mulches, fertilizers and even insect repellents. But most of them do not hesitate to use inorganic—but naturally occurring—materials, such as sand, ground limestone, and other rock derivatives, as long as they can do so without jeopardizing nature's tenuous balance.

At a time when products manufactured for chemical gardening, particularly those derived from petroleum, are becoming increasingly costly, organic gardening offers a common-sense way of growing safe, healthful foods, strong landscape plants and beautiful flowers, largely by recycling materials that might otherwise go to waste.

The use of natural gardening methods is not a fad; it is a simple, common-sense way to garden in partnership with nature. Many of the basic techniques of organic gardening, as a matter of fact, have long been used by all gardeners—advocates of organic and chemical means as well as ordinary green-thumbers. They include:

1) Balancing the soil's basic chemistry, adding limestone if it is too acid or sulfur if it is too alkaline.

2) Conditioning the soil by digging in organic matter, thus speeding drainage in a soil made too heavy by clay or slowing it in one made too light by sand. Chemicals cannot soften hardened soil or improve poor drainage; organic matter can.

3) Feeding the plants organically, primarily with nitrogen for lush green foliage, phosphorus for strong roots (especially in root crops such as beets and potatoes), and potassium (potash) for vigorous, disease-resistant growth. Of these three most essential nutrients, nitrogen demands the most constant monitoring because it cannot be taken from the air and it is quickly washed down beyond the root area. Also, it gets trapped at a critical time by soil bacteria if a certain type of mulch or compost (straw or other material with a high carbon-element content) is used.

Know Your Soil

An organic garden starts from the ground up. A rich, well-balanced soil is essential for growing strong plants of great variety, size, taste and color. Such soil is not difficult to achieve with processes that approximate, and improve upon, those that nature uses to improve the soil.

The pH factor. Soil is usually either alkaline (also called basic or sweet) or acid (sour), depending on its relative position on a chemical pH scale of 1 to 14. The pH is a measurement of hydrogen-ion concentration; soil with a pH of 7 is neutral, while the descending numbers indicate increasing acidity and the ascending numbers, an increasingly alkaline condition. Soil in most low rainfall areas is alkaline; in high rainfall areas it tends to be acidic (see map, page 1373, bottom, showing annual total rainfall in inches across the United States).

Many vines, shrubs and trees prefer a neutral soil; a few, such as rhododendrons, hollies, azaleas, and camellias prosper in a soil that is quite acid (pH of 4.5 to 5.5). Most vegetables and flowers grow best in soil that is neutral or only slightly acid (see soil acidity needs of plants, page 1362).

To neutralize soil that is too acid for the plants you want to grow, you can add ground limestone in a water solution or spread it lightly on the soil and allow it to leech into the ground. Soil that is too alkaline can be modified by adding ground sulfur-bearing rock, or by mulching or composting with material such as pine needles or oak leaves that are naturally acidic. The tables on page 1363 give amounts to use to achieve a near-neutral balance.

Charles Pfau was raised on a farm in Illinois, but he has been an urban farmer ever since his graduation from Columbia University in New York. As head gardener for philanthropist Stewart Mott's rooftop garden in Manhattan, he cares for nearly five hundred varieties of vegetables, fruits, flowers and herbs. He spends his weekends playing rugby, football, squash or tennis.

Planting marigolds among the cabbages as a natural pest control is a typical organic gardening method. For more on companion planting, including a listing of go-togethers, see pages 1367 and 1368.

SOIL ACIDITY NEEDS OF PLANTS

The approximate range of soil chemistry best suited to growth is given. Match soil type with plant variety for optimum results.

pH content	Trees, shrubs and vines	Flowers	Vegetables and fruits
Acid-sensitive plants (prefer neutral pH of 6.0 to 6.8)	Apple, apricot, arborvitae (American), ash (white, black, European mountain), Boston ivy, boxwood, Douglas fir, elm (American), flowering dogwood, hawthorn, lilac, oak (English), peach, pear, plum, sassafras, sugar maple, sycamore, tulip, walnut (black), willow, wisteria, witch hazel, yew	Begonia, carnation, cyclamen, delphinium, fern, fuchsia, geranium, lily, marigold, pansy, petunia, poinsettia, primrose, snapdragon, stock, sweet peas, yellow calla, zinnia	Asparagus, beets, carrots, cauliflower, celery, endive, leeks, lettuce, muskmelon, onions, parsnips, peas, spinach
Moderately acid-sensitive plants (prefer slightly acid pH of 5.5 to 6.8)	Clematis, Japanese flowering quince, red cedar	Rose	All beans, broccoli, brussels sprouts, cabbage, chard, cucumbers, eggplant, kale, kohlrabi, parsley, peppers, potatoes, pumpkins, radishes, rhubarb, squash, strawberries, sweet corn, sweet potatoes, tomatoes, turnips, watermelon
Slightly acid-sensitive plants (prefer moderately acid pH of 5.0 to 6.0)	Bayberry, beech, hemlock, holly (American, Japanese), juniper, mountain maple, mugho pine, oak (chestnut, pin, white, willow), spruce (Norway, red, sitka), Virginia creeper, winterberry		
Acid-loving plants (prefer acid pH of 4.5 to 5.5)	Azalea, bittersweet, blueberries, camellias, Colorado spruce, cranberries, heather, mountain laurel, red oak, rhododendron, white cedar, white pine	Gardenia; hydrangea (summer, pH 5.0 to 6.0), blue (winter, pH 5.0 to 5.8), pink (winter, pH 6.5 to 7.0)	

More detailed lists of plants are usually available at your local extension service. County agents can also arrange to have your soil tested to determine its acidity.

To determine the pH factor of the soil you intend to garden, you can test it yourself with a commercially available kit. To get a professional analysis, send samples taken from several parts of your garden to your state university, county agent, or a reputable testing service. Inquire first; there is usually a nominal charge. In return, you will receive a general analysis of your soil and recommendations for its improvement. Supplementary tests can also be run on request.

Soil structure. The texture of your soil is another vital consideration. Poor soil can be mostly clay—heavy, tightly packed, slow to drain (usually inland) or mostly sand—light, loose, quick to drain (usually near the seacoast). In spring, sandy soil warms up earlier than clay soil. Few soils are 100 percent clay or sand; most are somewhere between the extreme and the ideal.

Loam is soil with an ideal structure—crumbly, dark, rich in humus (organic matter), with good aeration and drainage. To achieve loam where it does not exist, you must dig organic matter into the existing soil, whether it is too sandy or too heavy with clay. Peat moss, available commercially, and homemade compost are most often used for this type of soil conditioning. In addition to improving the soil structure immediately, the organic matter provides important nutrients as it decays. Because it does decay though, in time it must be replenished.

Peat moss, compost and many other organic additives—sawdust, ground bark, aged manure, crop hulls, leaf mold—can be used to hold nutrient-bearing water long enough to nourish the plant without holding it so long that air is expelled and the plant drowns. Your county agent can advise you about locally available soil conditioners and their most effective usage.

The carbon/nitrogen ratio. Microorganisms share the soil with your plants and, in fact, are essential to plant health because they break down organic matter into a form that will nourish the plants. These microorganisms use the carbon in organic matter for energy and the nitrogen for growth. The relative amounts of carbon and nitrogen in the soil at any given time are measured by the soil's carbon/nitrogen ratio. Under normal conditions, this ratio is about 30 to 1; that is, roughly 30 parts of carbon to one part of nitrogen.

When organic material that is high in carbon and low in nitrogen (any dry, woody material such as straw or sawdust) is added to the soil, the desired balance of carbon and nitrogen is temporarily upset. The population of microorganisms explodes, depleting the nitrogen supply just at the time when the growing plants need it most. This condition is temporary, and in time the nitrogen will be returned to the soil by the decomposition of both the microorganisms and the organic material. But in the meantime, the plants suffer.

Since the high-carbon additives break down fast and release nutrients quickly, the answer is not to avoid them if they are available and inexpensive, but to supplement the nitrogen supply. This can be done with the high-nitrogen organic fertilizers discussed below. The balance can also be maintained by mixing the high-carbon additives with high-nitrogen organic materials—green grass clippings or kitchen wastes, leaves and leaf mold, peat moss, compost or manure. A third way to add nitrogen, much favored by commercial farmers, is to grow a legume crop—peas, beans, or especially soybeans—since legumes have root nodes that fix nitrogen in the soil.

Natural fertilizers. If an analysis of your soil (page 1362) indicates that it needs one of the three major nutrients—nitrogen, phosphorus or potassium (potash)—it can be supplied with organic materials that will be somewhat slow to take effect but for that very reason will be long lasting.

Nitrogen, as indicated above, is the most critical nutrient. Plants cannot take nitrogen from the air, but they must have it to produce abundant foliage. Thus, it is a particular necessity when you are growing leafy vegetables such as lettuce and spinach. Organic fertilizers that can be used to supply nitrogen include blood meal, hoof-and-horn meal, dried manure, various kinds of fish-based fertilizers, and cottonseed meal. Note that it is possible to overdo a good thing; too much nitrogen can produce such rapid growth that the plant is weak and susceptible to drought, disease and wind damage. In fact, it is possible to use too much of any fertilizer; it is a good idea to use a little less than the amount recommended on the package.

To supply added phosphorus, particularly needed for root crops, organic gardeners use bone meal or finely ground phosphate rock. The natural fertilizers that will supply potassium are wood ashes and ground granite or potash rock; such supplemental potassium is most often needed by plants grown for their flowers or fruit. Once a deficiency of phosphorus or potassium is corrected, the soil amendment should last for several years.

Any of these fertilizers which are packaged for commercial sale will have three numbers on the label, indicating the percentage of nitrogen, phosphorus and potassium they contain (in that order). Thus, you can tell at a glance that a package of blood meal (13-2-0) will be a valuable source of nitrogen, while bone meal (1-20-0) should be used to provide phosphorus.

Composting

Composting, one of the basics of organic gardening, is the process which returns organic matter to the soil. The compost, a mix of decayed and decaying plant life, is both a soil conditioner and a fertilizer. On uncultivated lands, composting is a natural process—leaves, grass and animal remains gradually decompose because of the actions of bacteria and weather, thus returning to the earth. The organic gardener only speeds this process.

The bacterial action needed to break down the plant fibers is aided by three things—heat, moisture and aeration—resulting in a dark, crumbling, sweet-smelling humus that is mixed with existing soil. Composting can take place in a small bucket, or in a pile that might contain several tons of material. The process can be completed in as little as two weeks or it can take several years.

To raise the soil's pH, decreasing its acidity, apply lime
Pounds of agricultural ground limestone needed per 1,000 square feet to raise pH:

Present pH of soil	(Sandy loam soils) to pH 6.0	or 6.5
6.0	none	23
5.5	23	46
5.0	46	69
4.8	55	78

Present pH of soil	(Silt loam soils) to pH 6.0	or 6.5
6.0	none	41
5.5	41	83
5.0	83	124
4.8	97	138

Present pH of soil	(Silty-clay loam soils) to pH 6.0	or 6.5
6.0	none	58
5.5	55	115
5.0	115	173
4.8	138	196

To lower the soil's pH, increasing its acidity, apply aluminum sulfate (or other sulfur product)
Pounds of aluminum sulfate needed per 100 square feet to lower pH:

Present pH of soil	to pH of	Pounds of aluminum sulfate
7.0	6.5	2.5
7.0	6.0	5.5
7.0	5.5	9.0
7.0	5.0	13.0
6.5	6.0	3.0
6.5	5.5	6.5
6.5	5.0	10.5
6.0	5.5	3.5
6.0	5.0	7.5
5.5	5.0	4.0

The tables above and the lists opposite were prepared by the Cooperative Extension Associations of Long Island, New York.

1: Compost begins with kitchen waste, spent flowers, stalks, leaves, grass clippings, and other organic matter. Small pieces aid decomposition.

2: At the halfway point, partially-decayed organic matter looks like this. Three things are needed for proper decomposition—heat, moisture and air.

3: The end result is rich, black, crumbling, sweet-smelling humus which is both a soil conditioner and a natural fertilizer.

To build a good compost pile, you must consider five basic points:

1. The texture of the raw organic materials. The smaller the particles, the faster decomposition will take place since more surfaces are available for bacteria to act on. However, when the material is too finely pulverized, the pile tends to become a solid, airless mass, inhibiting decomposition. To keep the pieces small, break up all the material you can by hand, with hand tools or with a mechanical grinder that shreds and cuts materials to the proper size. Leaves can be reduced to small flakes with a rotary lawn mower equipped with a leaf catcher.

2. The amount of moisture. A compost pile should always be moist—about the wetness of a squeezed-out sponge—but never soggy. The wetter the pile, the more you have to turn it to maintain good aeration. Wet dry stalks and dry grass as you add them to the pile; green materials usually need no additional water to start. In periods of heavy rainfall, you may want to cover the pile with canvas or plastic to keep it from getting too soggy.

3. The height of the pile. One factor that determines the temperature of the pile is its height. If it is too low, the pile loses heat rapidly; if too high, the materials are smothered by their own weight, a condition leading to a sour smell. A height between 4 and 6 feet is ideal. As the materials decompose, a 5-foot heap will shrink in volume to 3 or 3½ feet. In most climates, the air temperature does not affect the heat build-up in a properly prepared pile, so decomposition continues all winter.

4. The amount of nitrogen present. Decay-producing bacteria need nitrogen to work. If you are composting materials high in carbon, such as twigs or wood chips, add green grass clippings or organic fertilizers to provide easily decomposed sources of nitrogen (see carbon/nitrogen ratio, page 1363).

5. The need for turning the pile. Turning the pile occasionally loosens the materials which may have packed down, introduces more oxygen, and lets you re-distribute the pile so that the outer, less decomposed parts can be moved to the warmer center where they will decompose faster.

There are several methods of composting, but the most widely used method layers different materials so decomposition takes place more quickly and completely than it would if any one material were used.

A basic compost heap starts with 5 or 6 inches of garden and kitchen remains. You can even include the lint from a clothes dryer and the contents of a vacuum cleaner bag; they add valuable fine dust. When you save kitchen wastes for composting, use any vegetable matter that is not greasy. But remove seeds if you do not want to find strangers in your vegetable patch or flower bed at some future date. On top of the first layer, add a thin layer of manure or other nitrogen-rich fertilizer and a thin layer of topsoil, ground limestone, other rock powder or wood ashes. Moisten these layers with water and repeat them until a height of about 5 feet is reached. Form a shallow basin shape on top to catch rainwater, and cover the pile with a final layer of loose topsoil to retard evaporation. If an inexpensive thermometer is buried inside with a string to the outside, you can check the interior temperature in a few days. It should reach 140 to 160 degrees Fahrenheit; if it doesn't, add more water or nitrogen-rich matter.

The pile should be contained in a cage of chicken wire or an open, slatted wood box; no top or bottom is needed. If it is not contained, it will tend to spread out and become too thin. Decomposition is aided by the presence of oxygen; an open cage allows air to circulate. It also helps maintain a more even temperature at the edges of the pile. Building the pile on slats about 10 inches above the ground will also improve air movement. Stakes stuck into the pile as it is built, then pulled out, aerate it initially. After that, turning the pile will eliminate the unpleasant odor that occurs when the pile is moist but airless and cool.

The pit composting method works if you want to conceal the compost pile. Dig a hole about 3 feet deep and at least 4 feet square. Put into the pit as many organic materials as you can, making a compost heap below ground. Add layers of manure, straw, grass clippings, rock fertilizers, kitchen wastes, leaves; cover it finally with straw or hay. Such compost will have a high humus content and good texture. Decomposition will take longer, however, since air circulation is limited.

Sheet composting is the method by which you spread organic matter over soil that needs improvement and dig it in. The decomposition takes place right in the soil. This is best done in autumn, using fallen leaves, grass clippings, or other non-woody materials. By spring, the soil will be ready for planting.

The 14-day composting method was developed at the University of California and involves more intensive work. The raw materials must be finely chopped, with each piece an inch or less in diameter. The pile must be thoroughly turned every 2 or 3 days without fail to insure maximum aeration. Best results follow when the raw materials have a carbon/nitrogen ratio of about 30 to 1. The height of the heap should be between 3 and 4 feet, and the moisture content should be maintained at that of a squeezed-out sponge. This speeded-up compost piling method works best in a warm climate, and when all conditions are met properly.

The compost cocktail is one way you can benefit from composting, even if you don't have a backyard garden. This simple liquid mix is meant to be poured into the soil around your house plants or in a small container garden about twice a month. Collect scraps from your kitchen—egg shells, coffee grounds, tea leaves, potato peelings, fruit pulp, and other such waste. Mix them together in a food blender, add a little water to thin the mixture, and pour.

The Benefits of Mulching

Mulching is a labor-saving technique designed to keep soil temperatures constant around plant roots, retain moisture in the soil, prevent erosion, discourage weed growth and the spread of disease, and in the case of organic mulches, add nutrients to the soil. Non-organic mulches such as sand or gravel will not add nutrients to the soil, but they are effective in other respects. In winter a deep blanket of snow is one of the best natural mulches for protection of the soil and seeds below. Common organic mulches are listed on the following page.

An organic mulch should be about 6 inches deep when it is applied; as it decomposes, it will improve soil fertility and texture. In a vegetable garden, you can spade old mulches into the ground each year, and in the spring, spread a new layer. In this way, the constantly decomposing matter keeps the topsoil in prime condition. Mulches should be deeper around trees and shrubs with larger root systems than around flowers or vegetables. Although a mulch slows evaporation and thus helps the soil retain moisture, you will still need to water during dry periods. A mulch may make the soil too moist for seedlings, encouraging rot, so it is wise to wait several weeks after planting seedlings before mulching around them.

Mulching also aids sanitation by stifling diseases and over-winter parasites. In the early spring, pick off old leaves still clinging to diseased plants, remove any newly-infested leaves, and prune to remove infected branches. Dispose of these diseased parts; do not put them on the compost pile. Then apply a 2- or 3-inch thick mulch over the whole, clean bed. This must be done early; applying mulch after infections appear does little good in halting disease. The mulch acts as an insulating layer to keep soil-borne infectious materials from reaching the new growth. One of the best mulches for this purpose is a thick layer of well-rotted cow manure. Do not use fresh cow manure or chicken manure; both are high in nitrogen and may burn plants if applied as a thick mulch. Fallen leaves are commonly put in an organic

Pumpkins are easy to grow, thrive in hot weather, and can be stored for winter use. Roasted pumpkin seeds are a tasty, nutritious snack.

1365

MULCHING GUIDE

Common organic mulches	Advantages	Cautions
Straw or hay	Long lasting; attractive. Fine salt hay is less likely to blow around than finer-textured mulches	Both are low in nitrogen; you may need to add nitrogen to the soil to compensate for what the mulch takes out
Dry leaves	Found material; available in quantity for fall mulching	Should be dug into the soil after a year or two so the mulch does not become a breeding ground for insects
Coffee grounds	Found material; good for house plants	Generally available only in small quantities; unpleasant odor if not in solution
Grass clippings	Found material; fairly rich in nitrogen	Use before seed ripens; otherwise weeds and lawn grass may be introduced into planting area
Manure	Excellent; generally high nitrogen percentages; relatively odorless when dry	If too fresh, it can burn plants or may contain toxic nitrate concentrations
Peat moss	Excellent; absorbs and holds water well; aerates soil	If dry, you need to add water before using it as a mulch; tends to cake and shed water
Pine needles	Found material; long lasting; good around acid-loving plants	If too dry, can be a fire hazard
Leaf mold	Excellent for maintaining or increasing acidity	Expensive unless found material
Compost	Good texture; inexpensive if you have a compost heap	The finer, crumbling compost is more valuable for soil conditioning
Sawdust	Easy to handle; good cover; fine and dense so that 2 inches may be equivalent to 6 inches of straw or hay	Low in nitrogen; you may need to add nitrogen to soil to compensate for what the mulch takes out
Corn stalks	Found material; good aeration	Low in nitrogen; may harbor hidden pests

garden's compost heap to be used in the spring as compost, but they can also be used in the fall to mulch around plants. Applied *after* the ground has frozen, such a mulch will prevent the heaving of alternate freezing and thawing that damages roots. In the vegetable garden, spread the mulch of leaves from 6 to 8 inches deep over as much area as it will cover. When you get ready to plant in the spring, the soil underneath will be ready for you. For row crops, simply turn back the leaves along the row, exposing the rich, friable soil. Rake the soil a little, sow the seeds, cover them lightly, tamp, and cover lightly again, leaving the surface soil loose. For small seeds, make the furrow with the end of the hoe or rake handle; for large seeds, use the corner of the hoe. Leave the mulch turned back until seedlings are well established. Potatoes, however, can be re-covered at once with the leaves; the sprouts will find their way up through even a thick layer of mulch and little cultivation to control weeds will be necessary.

Friends, Not Foes

Crawling and flying creatures can be a problem around the garden, but some are among your garden's best friends. The praying mantis, ladybug, and earthworm are at the top of the list. Earthworms, as they burrow and feed, aerate the soil and help to decompose the organic materials. Praying mantises and ladybugs are the watchdogs of the garden, eating many harmful insects including mites and aphids. Praying mantis egg cases, earthworms and ladybugs can be ordered by mail.

Many birds, too, are insect eaters; lure them to your garden with houses, birdbaths and lumps of suet. Turtles and toads eat cutworms, aphids and white flies. It is said that a small Fowler's toad can eat its weight in insects each day. Fences and scarecrows forestall to some extent the marauding raids of rabbits, racoons, deer, woodchucks and other vegetarians.

Some vegetables seem to have a resistance to insects, among them carrots, beets, endive, onions, garlic, chives, okra, parsley, peppers, rhubarb, and usually lettuce. Above all, remember that a strong and healthy plant is less likely to succumb to an insect attack than one that is weak and undernourished.

The fierce-looking praying mantis is a guardian of your garden, eating harmful insects. Egg cases can be purchased from mail-order suppliers.

Organic Pesticides

Chemical poisons are not necessary to keep the bugs in your garden in check; various household items are more or less effective as pest controls. However, be realistic and do not expect them to be 100 percent successful. Wash any vegetables treated with these organic bug repellents before eating them. Even something that sounds as innocent as green soap can cause adverse reactions in some instances.

Saucers filled with beer and set out in the evening will trap and drown slugs. If the grasshopper population gets out of control, you can trap them with a 10 percent solution of molasses—fill a 2-quart jar half full and put it where they are most numerous. Dust plant leaves with garlic or onion salt from your spice rack, especially right after a rain when the leaves are still wet. Dusting tomatoes with ground-up hot peppers repels the green hornworm. Many bugs can simply be picked off by hand and destroyed; if the thought of touching bugs isn't appealing, wear gloves or use a paper towel. A strong stream of water from the garden hose is effective in some cases, washing tiny pests such as aphids far away from home.

Non-toxic sprays give you an easy way to attack many pests. Try to spray only infested plants, using a hand-held pressure sprayer. A simple all-purpose spray can be made from extracts of various plants. Select those with strong, sharp odors, such as hot peppers, onions, garlic and the heavy-smelling varieties of marigolds. Blend equal amounts of plant material and water in a food blender; strain out the plant remains; dilute this liquid extract in water (one teaspoon to a pint of water).

Aphids and white flies can be discouraged from living on your prized vegetables with a blend of garlic or onion juice, shredded tobacco, and liquid green soap. Strain, and pour or spray this solution on your plants. The ingredients and amounts can be varied. But do not omit soap; it makes the mixture stick to the leaves, remaining there to repel those insects returning after the initial burst of spray.

Companion Planting

What the ladybugs, birds and sprays miss, companion planting may catch—that is, mixing plants in such a way that one benefits from the other's company. Again, none of these organic methods is totally effective, but the benefits are noticeable.

Certain plants produce scents, oils or colors that either attract or repel various insects and animals. Plant these among your vegetables or near any plants you want to protect, either interspersing them in the same row, using them as a border, or planting them side by side in double zigzag rows.

Plants of the onion family (including garlic) are excellent insect, mice and mole repellents; some gardeners believe they improve the flavor of plants in their vicinity. Marigolds and nasturtiums are good insect repellents throughout the garden, especially the strong-smelling varieties. There is some evidence that marigolds reduce the number of weeds around them, too. Marigold roots are toxic to many bugs, and they are very effective against nematodes. Spent marigold plants are useful in a mulch around chrysanthemums and clematis vines; they repel bean beetles and Japanese beetles, too. Nasturtiums planted near vine plants such as lima beans help control aphids on those plants. A border of wormwood, yarrow or other strong-smelling herb will act as a scent fence. Mustard plants near cabbages will lure pests to themselves, where they can be removed.

Geraniums (particularly the white ones) and odorless marigolds are lure plants, attracting Japanese beetles away from other plants such as corn and roses. They stun the beetles so they can be picked off and drowned in a pail of water with a film of kerosene on top. The herb tansy can be rubbed on your arms to deter flying insects during evening work in the garden. Striped beetles, which prefer tender seedlings, can be thwarted by planting rings of radishes around the seedlings. Strong-smelling tomatoes repel the asparagus beetle; plant them with asparagus.

In addition to pest control, companion planting has other benefits. Plants with deep root systems enlarge the feeding area of plants with shallow root systems. Cabbage grows well near aromatic plants, but not near the tomato (also a heavy feeder). Lettuce, carrots and radishes (a great salad combination) can be grown in one container because each one feeds at a different soil depth. Soybeans are beneficial anywhere, as they fix nitrogen from the air and improve the soil. The herb fennel, however, will die in the presence of any close neighbor.

Companion planting could mean gardening with a friend, as this delightful etching shows. But to an organic gardener it means interplanting certain vegetables and flowers that benefit one another in some way, such as repelling harmful insects or deepening the feeding area for plants with shallow root systems.

COMPANION PLANTING GUIDE

Plant	With	But not with
Asparagus	Basil, eggplant, parsley, peppers, tomatoes	
Beans	Most vegetables and herbs	Garlic, gladioli, onions
Bush beans	Harsh-smelling marigolds or nasturtiums, savory, potatoes	Onions
Pole beans	Corn (to climb on)	Beets, kohlrabi, onions, sunflowers
Beets	Kohlrabi, onions	Pole beans
Cabbage family (broccoli, brussels sprouts, cabbage, cauliflower, kale, kohlrabi)	Aromatic plants and herbs (mint, rosemary, thyme), beets, celery, mustard, onions, potatoes	Pole beans, strawberries, tomatoes
Carrots	Chives, leaf lettuce, leeks, onions, peas, rosemary, sage, tomatoes	Dill
Celery	Bush beans, cabbage, cauliflower, leeks, tomatoes	
Chives	Carrots, lettuce	Beans, peas
Corn	Beans, cucumbers, geraniums, odorless marigolds, peas, potatoes, pumpkins, squash	Peppers, tomatoes
Cucumbers	Beans, corn, peas, radishes, sunflowers	Aromatic herbs, potatoes
Eggplant	Asparagus, basil, beans	Do not plant where tomatoes, potatoes or eggplant have been grown within the past three years
Fennel	Nothing	
Leeks	Carrots, celery, onions	
Lettuce	Chives, cucumbers, garlic, strawberries; carrots, radishes and lettuce are a super salad combination when grown together	
Onions (including garlic)	Beets, camomile (sparsely), lettuce, strawberries, summer savory, tomatoes	Beans, peas
Parsley	Asparagus, tomatoes	
Peas	Most vegetables and herbs	Garlic, gladioli, onions, potatoes
Peppers	Asparagus, basil	Corn
Potatoes	Beans, cabbage, corn, eggplant, horseradish (at corners of the patch), marigolds	Cucumbers, pumpkins, raspberries, squash, sunflowers, tomatoes
Pumpkins	Corn	Potatoes
Radishes	Carrots, cucumbers, lettuce, nasturtiums, peas, squash	
Soybeans	Anything	
Spinach	Strawberries	
Squash	Corn, nasturtiums, radishes	
Strawberries	Bush beans, lettuce (as a border), spinach	Cabbage; do not plant in any area where eggplant, melons, potatoes, raspberries or tomatoes have grown in the past three years or grass has grown in the past year
Sunflowers	Cucumbers	Potatoes
Tomatoes	Asparagus, basil, borage, carrots, chives, garlic, marigolds, nasturtiums, onions, parsley	Cabbage, corn, potatoes; do not plant in last year's potato patch if potatoes were infested with flea beetles
Turnips	Peas	

A rabbit would have a field day if he were allowed to roam freely in this container garden of leafy greens, but this one is a pet. From the left are carrot tops, Bloomsdale spinach and lettuce.

What to Plant

Organic gardening is concerned with what happens to the soil before the seeds are sown and with how to keep the growing plants healthy. In an organic garden, you plant the same vegetables and flowers you would find in any garden; there are no special "organic" plants and no "organic" ways to put the seeds in the ground. So if you are starting an organic vegetable garden, the important thing is to plant what you like. Then you will give your plants the care and attention they need to thrive. An organic garden cannot be a neglected garden; it may need more attention than one controlled with synthetic chemicals. If you are a beginner, start small— perhaps with just the makings of a season-long salad. Next year, add a few more vegetables, and so on. If space is really at a premium or if you are gardening in containers, consider miniature varieties. You can grow stalks of corn only 3 feet high with ears 4 inches long or heads of lettuce the size of baseballs.

Any of the vegetables you grow can be planted as seeds. Some can be started indoors and set out in your garden as seedlings or small plants, or you can purchase seedlings at plant stores. If seeds are so small they are difficult to sow, mix them with a little sand first. Onions are unusual in that they can be bought as seeds, as small plants, or as sets—which are tiny bulbs. The sets are easier and faster to grow than seeds, can be kept for a long time in a cool, dry place, and provide both green onions (scallions) and cooking onions. Berries and a few slow-growing vege- tables such as peppers and tomatoes are best bought as small plants. If you purchase seeds by mail, make sure the company guarantees its products; most do.

As you plan your garden, you may be dealing with annuals, perennials and biennials. An annual is a plant that grows, produces seed and dies in a single season; it must be replanted each year. Most vegetables are annuals. A perennial lives and blooms year after year, often dying to the ground in fall and coming up from the roots in spring. Asparagus is a perennial. Flowering perennials begin blooming the second year from seed. A biennial produces roots and leaves the first year, blooms and seeds the second year, then dies. Carrots and parsley are biennials; if you plant them for seed, harvest them at the end of the second season.

To keep vegetables coming, try succession planting—putting in a row or two every week or so until about two months before frost is expected. In this way, the plants won't all mature at once, and you can spread the harvest over the whole season. This works especially well with bush beans and other vine crops.

Most seeds lose their vitality within a year if they are not planted; check the germination date. If you can't plant the seeds you buy within a few weeks, store them in a cool, dry place such as your refrigerator.

When you plant, leave narrow paths at intervals, and mark each row with the name of the variety, the date planted, and the source. Use flat wooden sticks for labels and write with a waterproof marker. The following year, rotate the plants to keep any soil-borne disease from being passed on to the new crop.

Compost — **Sheet plastic**
Soil mix — **Pebbles**

Container

A

Figure A: A container ready for planting is layered with pebbles for drainage, sheet plastic (with slits) to keep the soil from filtering down, the soil mixture, and humus.

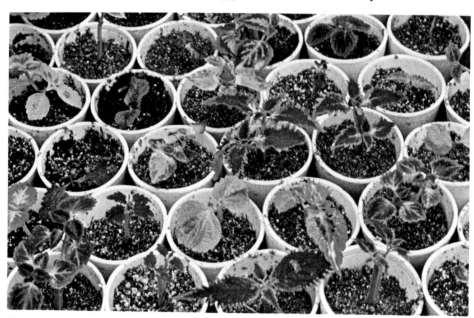

Plants can be grown in any container that holds soil and permits adequate drainage. Plastic foam cups with holes punched in the bottom are ideal for starting new plants, such as these coleus cuttings.

Containers

Gardening in containers gives you an ideal opportunity to experiment with organic gardening; you can give this mini-garden environment the close attention organic gardening requires, and easily follow the results of your work. Gardening in containers is especially practical if you have little or no yard space or very poor soil. Because they are relatively small, most containers usually can be moved from one spot to another, depending on the plant's need for sunlight or shade, or they can be brought indoors when a frost threatens. They also can be raised to any level with bricks, boxes or cinder blocks, allowing you to reach the vegetables without stooping or bending. Plants in containers require frequent watering; add organic materials to the potting soil and use a mulch to retard evaporation.

Plants will grow in any container that will hold soil and permit drainage—including plastic foam cups, coffee cans, discarded drawers, old tires, wicker baskets, clay pots, wooden tubs or metal planters. Metal will not rot or warp, but the outside surfaces should be painted with a rust-retardant paint if the container is to be left outdoors. To prevent rust on the inside, coat the metal with roofing tar. In some instances, a planter is specifically designed for a certain plant; the clay jar in the photograph, left, has many openings for strawberry plants. It can also be used for clusters of herbs.

Whatever container you use, it should be porous-bottomed or have drainage holes. Wooden boxes are rarely tight enough to pose a drainage problem. If you use a metal container, drill holes in the bottom or lower sides if they do not exist. In addition, put a layer of clay-pot shards, broken glass, broken bricks, gravel or pebbles in the container before you add the soil to create a drainage reservoir below the plant. Over the bottom layer, put plastic sheeting with occasional slits to keep

If space is limited, you can grow strawberries in a clay jar that has pockets all around to hold individual plants. This type of container can also be used to grow a variety of herbs in a small area.

the soil from filtering down but permitting drainage (see Figure A, opposite).

Potting soil. Even if you buy pre-packaged potting soil for container gardening, it needs help to reach its full potential. One definite advantage of such packaged soil is that it usually has been sterilized to kill insect larvae, weed seeds, fungi and bacteria that might harm your plants. However, you are bound to add some, as you modify the soil's structure. To the potting soil, add equal amounts of coarse builder's sand (sea sand is too salty), peat, and compost. For every bushel of the mix, add a pint or so of bone meal, which contains nitrogen and trace elements. Substitutes for compost, if you do not have it, include leaf mold (especially for acid-loving plants), aged sawdust mixed with leaf-mold, or well-rotted manure. Avoid fresh manure; it can burn plants in its ammonia-releasing stage and it may contain too much soluble nitrogen which may lead to toxic nitrate concentration.

Water, Air and Sun

Plants need water, air and light, but it is possible to have too much of a good thing. Be especially careful not to over-water; more plants are drowned than ever die of thirst. The best times to water your plants are early morning or evening; avoid the strong heat of midday. Use cool or tepid water, not cold. If you can, set out a tub to catch rainwater and use that, rather than the heavily chlorinated water found in many water systems. Avoid spraying the foliage of the plant with water, especially if it will not have time to dry before dark. Roses sprinkled in the evening are subject to attacks of mildew and black spot.

You will be an angel if you water your plants with tepid—not cold—water to avoid shocking them.

You can't give soil a once-over-lightly watering with good results. If you water just a little, only the top layer is dampened and the soil around the roots remains dry. You need to water the soil deeply; then let it alone until the top feels dry again.

Generally, leafy vegetables, including radishes, lettuce and herbs, can withstand the most shade, while flowers and fruits demand the most sunlight. Tomatoes need a lot of sunlight, too, and root vegetables fall somewhere in between.

Heat-loving plants are peppers, tomatoes, squash, pumpkins, corn and cabbage. Vegetables that prefer cool weather and can be planted in early spring or late fall are radishes, peas, lettuce and cabbage.

For related entries, see "Birds and Birdhouses," "Bottle Gardens," "Greenhouses," "Lighted Indoor Gardens," "Insects," and "Pickled and Canned Foods."

Vegetables harvested from an organic garden look good enough to eat—and they are. They were grown naturally, without the use of chemical fertilizers or poisonous pesticides.

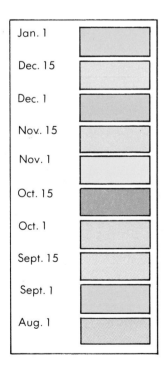

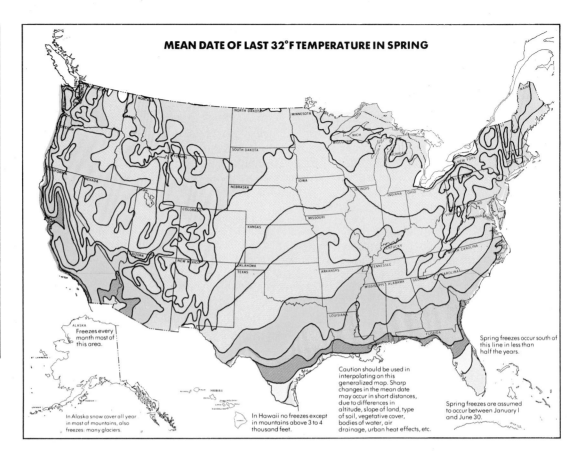

MEAN DATE OF LAST 32°F TEMPERATURE IN SPRING

ALASKA
Freezes every month most of this area.

In Alaska snow cover all year in most of mountains, also freezes: many glaciers.

In Hawaii no freezes except in mountains above 3 to 4 thousand feet.

Caution should be used in interpolating on this generalized map. Sharp changes in the mean date may occur in short distances, due to differences in altitude, slope of land, type of soil, vegetative cover, bodies of water, air drainage, urban heat effects, etc.

Spring freezes occur south of this line in less than half the years.

Spring freezes are assumed to occur between January 1 and June 30.

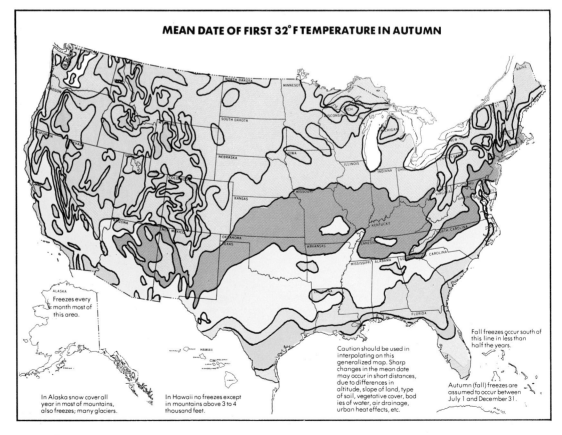

MEAN DATE OF FIRST 32°F TEMPERATURE IN AUTUMN

ALASKA
Freezes every month most of this area.

In Alaska snow cover all year in most of mountains, also freezes; many glaciers.

In Hawaii no freezes except in mountains above 3 to 4 thousand feet.

Caution should be used in interpolating on this generalized map. Sharp changes in the mean date may occur in short distances, due to differences in altitude, slope of land, type of soil, vegetative cover, bodies of water, air drainage, urban heat effects, etc.

Fall freezes occur south of this line in less than half the years.

Autumn (fall) freezes are assumed to occur between July 1 and December 31.

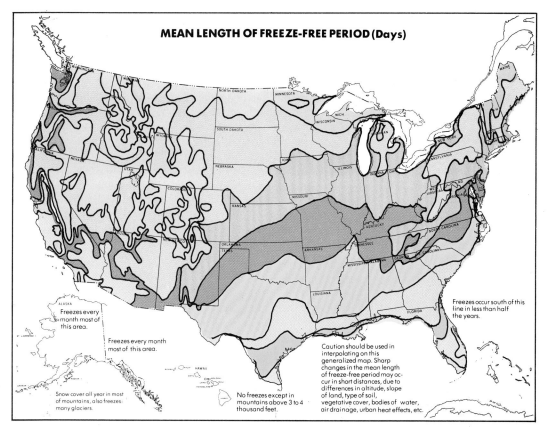

MEAN LENGTH OF FREEZE-FREE PERIOD (Days)

Freezes every month most of this area.

Freezes every month most of this area.

Snow cover all year in most of mountains, also freezes: many glaciers.

No freezes except in mountains above 3 to 4 thousand feet.

Freezes occur south of this line in less than half the years.

Caution should be used in interpolating on this generalized map. Sharp changes in the mean length of freeze-free period may occur in short distances, due to differences in altitude, slope of land, type of soil, vegetative cover, bodies of water, air drainage, urban heat effects, etc.

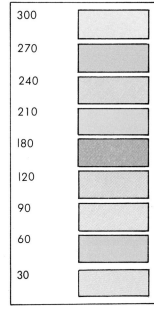

300
270
240
210
180
120
90
60
30

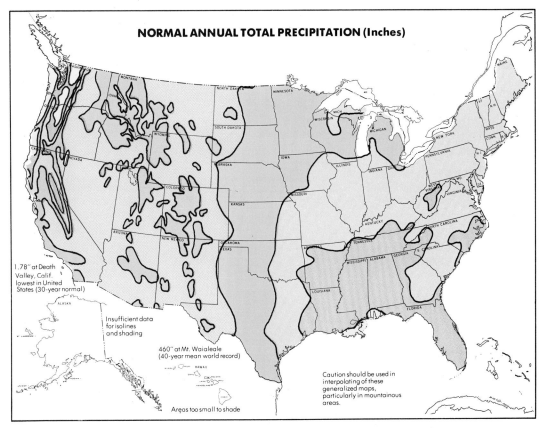

NORMAL ANNUAL TOTAL PRECIPITATION (Inches)

1.78" at Death Valley, Calif. lowest in United States (30-year normal)

Insufficient data for isolines and shading

460" at Mt. Waialeale (40-year mean world record)

Areas too small to shade

Caution should be used in interpolating of these generalized maps, particularly in mountainous areas.

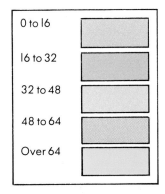

0 to 16
16 to 32
32 to 48
48 to 64
Over 64

Maps on both pages prepared by the National Weather Service, U. S. Department of Commerce.

Toshiko Takahara was born in Japan and works for the Japanese consulate in New York. She also teaches kindergarten in a Japanese school and sets aside time every month to help her class master the principles of origami.

ORIGAMI
Japanese Paper Folding

Origami, one of Japan's most charming and captivating exports, is more than a hobby or a craft. It is a folk art that has been a part of the Japanese culture for hundreds of years. These folded paper figures are not only decorative — many have been endowed with symbolic meanings. Noshi folds, for example, are simple figures customarily fastened on gifts to symbolize the giver's good wishes. The classic figure of the crane, pictured opposite, is symbolic of long life. The frog shown on page 1384 represents fertility and love.

As a popular Western pastime, origami's appeal lies in the fascination evoked by transforming a flat piece of paper into a three-dimensional form without so much as a drop of glue or the snip of a scissors. Children and computer programmers, mathematicians and science-fiction fans, engineers and writers, magicians and puzzle-solvers are all drawn by the magic of origami. Houdini wrote a book called *Houdini's Paper Magic* in which there was a section devoted to origami. Paper folding was one of Lewis Carroll's favorite diversions. According to his diary, he spent "a remarkable day" entertaining children of the Duchess of Albany by folding a paper pistol that actually went off with a loud crack when snapped through the air. This diverse group of origami aficionados have one thing in common: a love of ingenuity and imagination, two elements that, combined with elegance, are evident in even the simplest origami model.

Tools and Materials

No tools are required—even scissors are optional. Paper and a flat, hard surface on which to fold it are all you need to make an origami figure. Any paper that will hold a sharp crease can be used, but origami paper, imported from Japan and widely available, is especially recommended. This paper, white on one side and brightly colored on the other, comes in packages of squares that measure 4 to 7 inches on each side. Most origami figures start with a square of paper, so pre-cut squares are convenient. But since it is simple to cut or tear any rectangle into a square (see Craftnotes, left), the difference in the two sides of the paper is its primary attraction. This contrast between white and color is most effective and indeed is essential for such figures as the pinwheel (page 1379) and the penguin (page 1380).

If you cannot find origami paper in your area, other papers that can be used include gift-wrap paper (carrier pigeon on page 1382), shelf paper, brown wrapping paper, lightweight bond or typing paper (drinking cup, page 1378), and newspaper (samurai hat, page 1381). You might also like to experiment with waxed paper, foil, tissue paper, or tracing paper for special effects.

Procedure

Most origami figures are folded from a square piece of paper; the one exception in this entry is the carrier pigeon pictured on page 1382. If you are not starting with a pre-cut square, see the Craftnotes, left.

The chart of symbols given in the Craftnotes on page 1376 will help you interpret the directions and diagrams that follow on how to fold each origami figure. Unless otherwise indicated, the figure is diagrammed as it will look at the beginning of each step. The folds to be made are indicated by symbols and described in the captions. Make the folds as straight as you can; then crease them with a fingernail. Take time to fold accurately; the beauty of an origami figure comes from folds that are as close to perfect as possible.

Occasionally certain parts of the paper will be identified with a letter in the diagram. If this is your first experience with origami, copy these letters lightly onto the paper you are folding. This will help you keep track of the flaps after they are folded and change positions.

The crane is a traditional symbol of long life and good luck; according to Japanese folklore, the crane lives for 1,000 years. Each of these cranes was folded from a single 7-inch square of origami paper, without using scissors or glue. Directions for folding the crane are on page 1383.

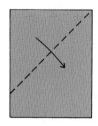
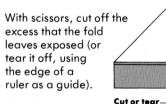
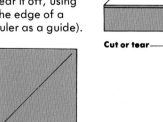

CRAFTNOTES: THE SYMBOLS OF ORIGAMI

— — — — — — —
Valley fold

— ·· — ·· — ·· —
Mountain fold

——————————
Existing crease

· · · · · · · · · · · · · ·
Previous position, future position, or X-ray view

Fold forward

Fold behind

Tuck in, open out, or apply force

Fold over and over

Turn model over

International origami symbols, consisting of a code of lines and arrows, were devised by Akira Yoshizawa, a master artist in this field. The parts of this code that are used in this entry are shown above.

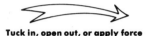
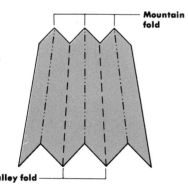
Mountain fold

Valley fold

The valley fold is the most common fold; fold the paper toward you so the dashed line, if drawn on the paper, would fall on the inside of a valley. The mountain fold is folded away from you; if the dot-and-dash line were drawn on the paper, it would fall on the outside of the paper, along the top of a ridge.

Shaded areas in the folding diagrams indicate the colored side of the paper. If you are using origami paper, this will help you make correct folds.

The projects that follow are presented in increasing order of difficulty. Begin with a simple figure to acquaint yourself with the techniques; then progress to the more complicated designs. You need not begin with the cat or dog face opposite, but you might have difficulty if you attempt the crane or the jumping frog before you have folded a few of the easier figures.

Paper Folding and Cutting
Dog face and cat face

Children, who know a good thing when they see it, quickly become fascinated with origami. In only a few minutes, even kindergarten children can turn a sheet of paper into a delightful image. The Japanese people have long used origami as a painless way to teach accuracy, patience and concentration, and to let children experience the pleasure of accomplishment. Although most Japanese adults can fold a few origami figures from memory, today the world of origami is inhabited largely by the children of Japan.

Teaching Origami
Origami teaching begins with simple figures. The dog face and cat face shown opposite are excellent projects for 5-year olds; older children will be able to handle the house, the cup, or the penguin on the pages that follow. If you are helping a child learn origami, make sure he has enough room and a work surface that is smooth and flat. Make up a model to show the students beforehand. Demonstrate, describing the steps as you go. Announce each goal in advance: "Now we will make an ear," or whatever the next step will be.

さあ　こんどは　みみを　おりましょう ("Now you have to fold the ear.")

Dog Face

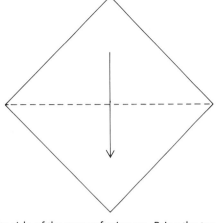

Step 1: Position the square of paper with the white side of the paper facing up. Bring the top corner down to the bottom, making a valley fold and forming a triangle.

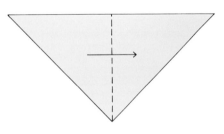

Step 2: Fold the triangle in half to find the center; then unfold it.

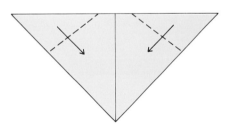

Step 3: Using the fold to locate the center, form the ears by folding the outer corners inward.

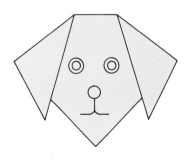

Step 4: The dog face is complete when you have drawn the face with a crayon.

Cat Face

Steps 1 and 2 are the same as steps 1 and 2 for the dog face.

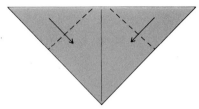

Step 3: Fold the ears closer to the center line than for the dog face.

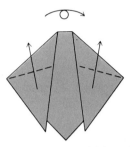

Step 4: Finish the ears by folding them upward as shown. Turn the model over.

Step 5: The cat face is complete when you have drawn the features with a crayon.

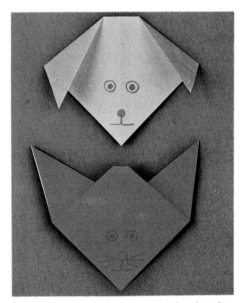

Learning to make both of these simple origami figures is easy because the folds used for the cat (bottom) are based upon those used for the dog.

Paper Folding and Cutting
Drinking cup

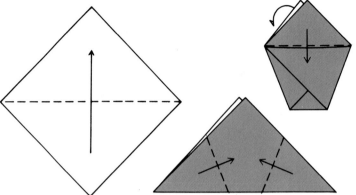

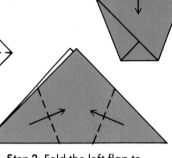

Step 1: Fold the bottom corner up to the top corner.

Step 2: Fold the left flap toward the right and the right flap toward the left.

Step 3: Fold the front top flap forward and the back top flap behind.

Step 4: The drinking cup is completed.

A square of relatively heavy plain white paper, such as bond typing paper, works best when folding this origami drinking cup. It really holds cold liquids—but not forever, so bottoms up.

Paper Folding and Cutting
House

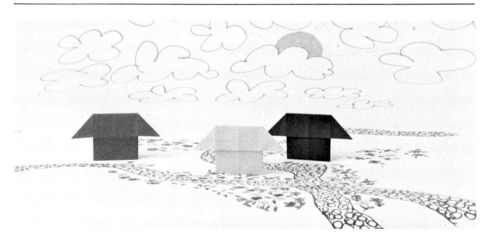

Here, a fantasy scene was drawn around an arrangement of real origami houses. In Japan, such houses are made with special sheets of paper on which doors, windows, and figures are printed.

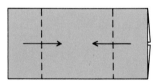

Step 3: Valley-fold the left and right edges so they meet at the center fold in front.

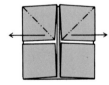

Step 4: To form the roof, pull the two upper flaps in an outward direction. Flatten them, as shown in step 5.

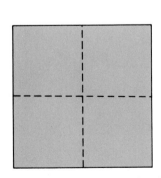

Step 1: With the colored side of the paper facing up, valley-fold it into quarters. This establishes the center folds which act as guides.

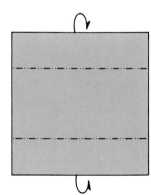

Step 2: Mountain-fold the top edge and the bottom edge so they meet at the center fold in back.

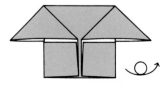

Step 5: The house is completed; turn the model over.

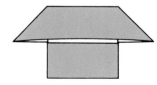

Step 6: The house is seen from the front. If you like, draw in windows and a door.

Paper Folding and Cutting
Pinwheel

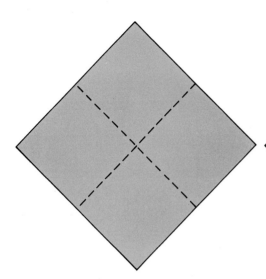

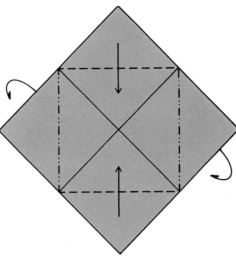

Step 1: Place the paper with the color side facing up. Valley-fold in quarters to establish the center lines.

Step 2: Valley-fold the top and bottom corners to the center front; mountain-fold the side corners to the center back.

A 6-inch square of paper, a dowel, a straight pin, a bead and a light hammer are all the supplies you need to make a pinwheel. To make pinwheels for use as Christmas decorations, see page 1385.

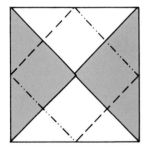

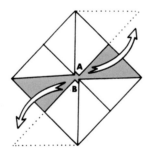

Step 3: Valley-fold two opposite corners to the center front; mountain-fold the two remaining corners to the center back.

Step 4: Pull out points A and B to the positions indicated by the dotted lines.

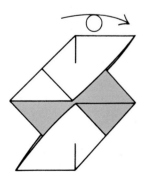

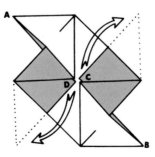

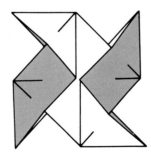

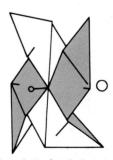

Step 5: Step 4 is shown completed; turn the pinwheel over.

Step 6: Pull out points C and D to the positions indicated by the dotted lines.

Step 7: The pinwheel is completely folded.

Step 8: To finish the pinwheel, attach it to a dowel or other stick by hammering in a straight pin, placing a bead in between for a spacer.

1379

Paper Folding and Cutting
Penguin

This penguin design is an example of how the contrast between the white and the color side of the origami paper can be used to advantage. To make a penguin family, use squares of paper in a sequence of sizes, such as one 4-inch, one 6-inch, and one 10-inch square.

Step 1: With the color side of the paper facing up, fold the bottom corner as shown.

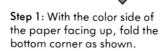

Step 2: Bring the right corner to the left corner, making a valley fold.

Step 3: To begin forming the first wing, valley-fold the top layer of the left flap to the front so it extends a bit beyond the center fold.

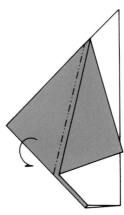

Step 4: To begin the second wing, mountain-fold the remaining left flap to the back.

Step 5: To form the head, valley-fold the top flap forward; then unfold it. Unfold the center fold slightly; grasp the top flap between thumb and index finger and pull it gently upward and outward. The flap will flip downward, forming a hood-like shape (see step 6).

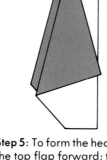

Step 6: Step 5 has now been completed.

Step 7: To finish folding the first wing, open it out as far as it will go. Valley-fold as shown; then push in (indicated by the arrow), and form the mountain fold (see step 8).

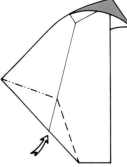

Step 8: The penguin is completely folded.

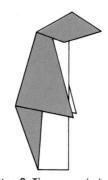

Paper Folding and Cutting
Samurai hat

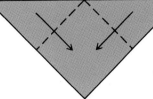
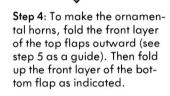
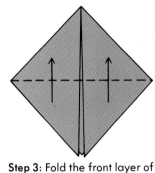

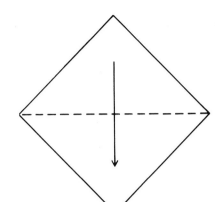

Step 1: Fold the top corner down to meet the bottom corner as shown.

Step 2: Fold the side flaps toward the center.

Step 3: Fold the front layer of the bottom flaps up.

Step 4: To make the ornamental horns, fold the front layer of the top flaps outward (see step 5 as a guide). Then fold up the front layer of the bottom flap as indicated.

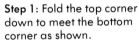
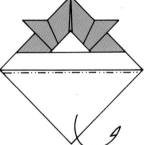
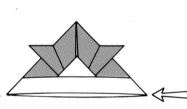
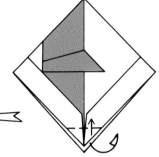

Step 5: Fold the bottom flap up again as shown.

Step 6: Fold the remaining layer of the bottom flap to the back (you may find it easier to turn the model over to do this).

Step 7: Push the corners toward each other until they meet (see step 8).

Step 8: Fold the two bottom corners up in front and in back. This will secure the previous folds.

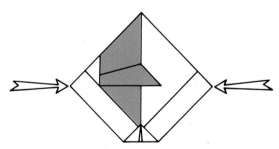

Step 9: Push the corners together as indicated, opening the hat as in step 7.

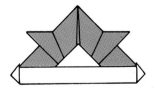

Step 10: The hat is completed.

These newspaper hats are based on a medieval Japanese helmet that featured horn-like ornaments. A 20-inch square of paper will make one child-sized hat; if newspapers measure less than 20 inches in your area, glue two sheets together; then cut or tear a square as shown on page 1374.

Carrier pigeon

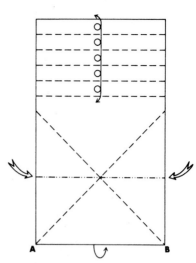

Step 1: Position a rectangle or paper with the white side facing up. Crease the bottom portion of the paper as indicated. Then write a message on the top portion of the rectangle, and fold down the upper edge again and again. Push in where indicated by the arrows.

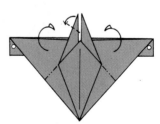

Step 7: Bring the cut edges of flap A together along the center line, and flatten A so that its tip touches the bottom point forming the mountain folds shown in step 6.

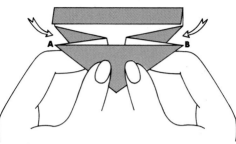

Step 2: Step 1 is shown in progress. Flatten the front and back (see step 3).

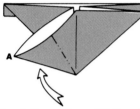

Step 4: To continue, lift flap A and squash it downward so its two sides are forced open, and form the mountain fold shown in step 3.

Step 5: Step 4 is shown in progress.

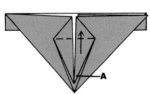

Step 8: The petal fold is shown completed. Lift flap A as far as it will go; then flatten it, making the valley fold indicated.

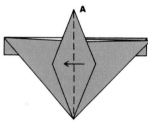

Step 9: Fold the right half of A over to the left.

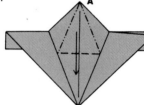

Step 3: Mountain-fold the message to the back. Make a squash fold with flap A as follows: begin by folding flap A to the right.

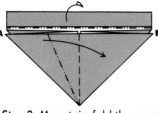

Step 6: The squash fold is shown completed. Petal-fold flap A as follows: begin by bringing the tip of flap A down to the bottom point.

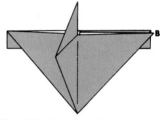

Step 10: Step 9 is shown completed. Repeat the squash fold, the petal fold, and steps 8 and 9 with flap B.

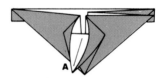

Step 11: Mountain-fold the two halves of the message so that their edges meet along the center back. Pierce or punch holes as indicated; then slip a string through the holes and tie the ends in a bow. To form the head, reverse-fold flap A as follows: valley-fold the tip to the front as indicated, and then unfold it.

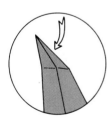

Step 12 (enlarged detail): Insert the thumb between the folds of the head and push to the right while pushing down with the index finger. The creases will reverse themselves.

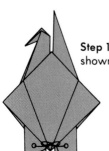

Step 13: The carrier pigeon is shown completed.

The message within this origami carrier pigeon remains concealed until the recipient unfolds it.

Paper Folding and Cutting
Crane

¢ ⊠ ♟ 🐿

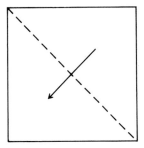

Step 1: Position the paper with the white side facing up. Valley-fold the paper diagonally in half, forming a triangle.

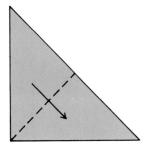

Step 2: Valley-fold the triangle as indicated.

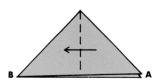

Step 3: Valley-fold the front layer of Flap A, then unfold. Open up the flap and flatten it to form the square you see in step 4. This brings the tip of flap A over to B.

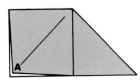

Step 4: Step 3 is shown completed. Turn the model over and repeat step 3 behind.

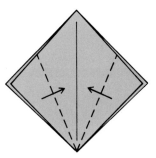

Step 5: With the square open at the bottom, valley-fold the front layer of the side flaps toward the center.

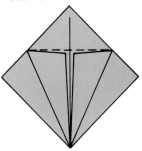

Step 6: Valley-fold the top flap down. Unfold the model so it looks like step 5.

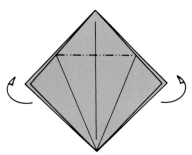

Step 7: Repeat steps 5 and 6 behind.

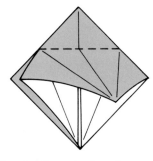

Step 8: Lift up the front layer of the bottom flap making a valley fold as indicated. Push in at the sides of the flap so the cut edges meet along the center front; flatten it into a diamond shape (see step 9). This step is rather difficult, and the paper will need to be coaxed gently into shape.

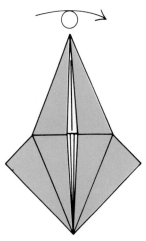

Step 9: Step 8 is shown completed. Turn the model over and repeat step 8 behind.

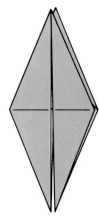

Step 10: Step 8 is shown completed on front and back.

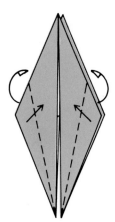

Step 11: Valley-fold the front layer of the side flaps to the center. Repeat behind.

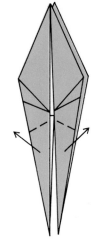

Step 12: Reverse-fold the tail and neck sections upward (see carrier pigeon step 12).

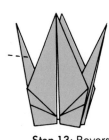

Step 13: Reverse-fold the head downward as indicated. To complete the model, gently pull apart the wings so the body of the crane opens up and takes on a three-dimensional form.

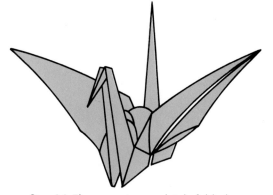

Step 14: The crane is completely folded (see photograph on page 1375).

1383

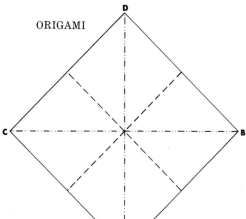

Step 1: Position the paper with the white side facing up. Valley-fold into quarters; then mountain-fold diagonally.

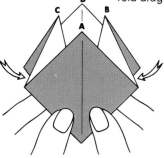

Step 2: Push C and B together until they meet. Flatten flaps A and D. Turn the model around so the folded point is at the top.

Jumping frog

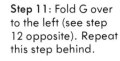

It's only a paper frog floating on a paper pond, but if you know the secret, you can make him almost come to life, much to the delight of children and grown-ups alike. To make the frog jump, stroke his back gently, and let your finger slip off and snap onto the table.

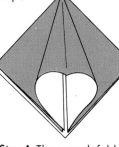

Step 4: The squash fold is shown in progress.

Step 5: Fold the lower edges of the flap toward the center line.

Step 3: Make a squash fold (see carrier pigeon, steps 3, 4 and 5) with the front layer of the right flap.

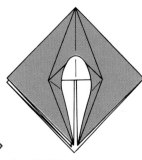

Step 7: This shows step 6 in progress. Flatten the edge upward, forming a point, and bring the raw edges together at the center front.

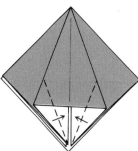

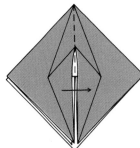

Step 8: Fold the left half of the flap over the right half. Repeat from step 3 with the front layer of the left flap. Turn the model over and repeat steps 3 through 8.

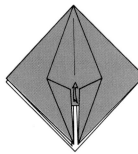

Step 6: Unfold the last step slightly, grasp the hidden edge, and pull it up as far as it will go.

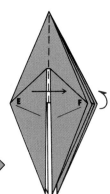

Step 9: Step 8 is shown enlarged and completed. Bring E over to F, revealing a smooth surface in front. Repeat behind.

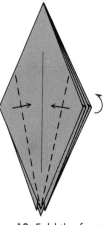

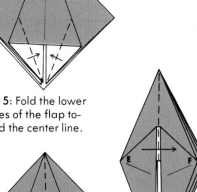

Step 10: Fold the front layer of the lower edges to the center line. Repeat behind and on the sides (see step 11).

Step 11: Fold G over to the left (see step 12 opposite). Repeat this step behind.

Paper Folding and Cutting
Uses of origami

Although they may be enjoyed just as they are, origami figures can be put to many decorative uses. Large sheets of paper can be folded into oversized figures for display as sculpture or as party centerpieces. Many figures are suitable for use in a mobile or as Christmas tree ornaments (below); flatter figures may be glued to folded pieces of paper to make unique greeting cards.

For related crafts and projects, see "Airplanes of Paper," "Greeting Cards," "Mobiles," "Papermaking," "Silhouettes," and "Valentines."

These pinwheels, made from squares of double-faced paper (two sheets of different colors rubber-cemented together), were folded following the directions on page 1379, embellished with pre-gummed stars and suspended by a length of doubled thread knotted at the end. The red crane (folding directions are on page 1383) was hung with a length of doubled thread passed through the center of the body.

To make a crane mobile, pass a doubled, knotted thread through the center of each crane body; tie a knot with each thread around the inside ring of an embroidery hoop, and join at the top with a knot.

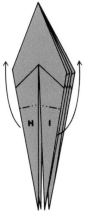

Step 12: Reverse-fold H and I up as far as possible. (See carrier pigeon, step 12, for reverse fold.)

Step 13: Reverse-fold J and K as indicated.

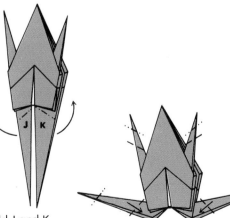

Step 14: Finish the front and rear legs by making the valley and mountain folds indicated.

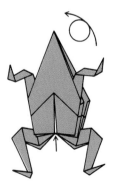

Step 15: Blow into the small opening at the bottom to inflate the frog slightly. Turn the model over.

Step 16: The completed frog is shown.

PAPERMAKING
A Beautiful Beginning

Kathryn and Howard Clark operate the Twinrocker Handmade Paper workshop in Brookston, Indiana, where they make custom papers for artists, printmakers and bookbinders. Howard, an engineer and industrial designer, is director of Twinrocker. Kathryn, a printer, directs the Purdue University Center for Handcrafted Papers. The Clarks have lectured across the country and exhibited their works at museums and galleries, including the Museum of Contemporary Crafts in New York and the Indianapolis Museum of Art. In 1974 they received the American Craftsmen Grant from the National Endowment for the Arts.

Did you know you can make paper at home? Imagine binding a diary with pages of handmade paper, or framing an original drawing that you have done on paper you made. A poem or a recipe given to a friend will mean more if it is on paper you created with loving care.

Most of the paper used today is made of wood pulp in large mills. But these papers—newspapers, store wrappings, cereal boxes, notebook papers, paper towels, junk mail, magazine pages, typing paper—can be broken down again into pulp in your food blender and turned into clean new sheets for craft projects, party invitations and greeting cards, or children's artwork.

The finest and most durable papers, including currency, stock and bond certificates and most business letterhead paper, are made entirely or partially of rag or cotton-fiber pulp. Recycled rag paper can also be made at home as a beautiful beginning for other creative ventures.

What Is Paper?

Paper is cellulose, which comes only from plant or vegetable fibers. Most plants (including trees) contain substances other than cellulose and therefore are not suitable for fine paper unless the other substances are removed.

Cotton is 95 percent cellulose; because cotton fibers are more profitably made into fabrics, the raw fibers are rarely used in paper. Until recently, most rag paper was made from just that—worn-out rags—because cellulose is not affected by years of washing and wearing. The extensive use of synthetic fibers in fabric has changed that, so mills making rag paper to a large extent now use new cloth remnants from clothing manufacturers, plus cotton linters, a fuzz of short fibers that clings to cottonseeds after they are ginned. Chemicals are not needed in the production of rag paper.

The fibers used in papermaking should be long, and cotton fibers are extremely long, thin and twisted, making them very flexible. Linen is similar to cotton but the fibers are thicker and straighter, so paper with a high percentage of linen is stiff and strong. Hemp, jute and manila fibers are used in coarse, heavy papers.

Tree fibers are longer than those of most plants, but the longest wood fibers are only about five percent as long as cotton or linen fibers. And they are only 50 percent cellulose; the other 50 percent is lignin, which binds the fibers together, and resin. It is possible to make paper of lesser quality from wood without removing these substances, and such pulp is the main ingredient in newsprint. Lignin oxidizes rapidly, however; it is what makes newspaper clippings turn yellow and brittle. Most wood pulp used for paper has the lignin removed chemically, but some of the chemicals may remain behind and affect the life and the looks of the paper. Standard typing paper is an example of a better-grade wood-pulp paper.

A

Figure A: The first paper was made in China; this is the Chinese symbol for paper.

Special notes call for special stationery, perhaps of rag paper that you have made by hand. Instructions for making rag paper like this begin on page 1394 The unfolded envelope is shown on page 1396 . The old engraving shows a European paper mill of the mid 1600's.

What Papers Are Not Paper?

Papyrus was around long before paper, but it is not a true paper, since it is not macerated, but laminated from strips of the papyrus stalk. Rice paper as we know it is not made from rice, but from the inner bark of the paper mulberry tree, grown in the Orient. It resembles paper made from rice straw. Real parchment and vellum, which are still available and used by bookbinders, are made from animal skins; commercially available parchment and vellum papers are types that simulate the originals. Linen paper, too, is usually a paper given a surface finish that resembles linen cloth and is not a paper made of linen fibers.

How Is Paper Made?

The way in which paper is formed has changed very little in almost 2,000 years. The first paper was made in 105 A.D. in China, where the process was kept secret for hundreds of years. Before then, writing and painting were done on bamboo scrolls and silk. Paper was finally introduced into Europe in the twelfth century, and its use became widespread by the fifteenth century. Earlier, vellum and parchment were used in Europe, and paper was first called cloth parchment. The first papermaking mill in America started in 1690 near Philadelphia, and until the 1850's, most paper was made by hand. The use of wood pulp began in the late 1800's. Today, the United States is the world's largest producer of paper.

Cellulose fibers alone cannot be made into paper; they must be thoroughly macerated with water until each filament is a separate unit, swollen and suspended in water. Paper pulp is roughly 95 percent water and five percent fiber. A mortar and a pestle, and later a stamping mill, were used to macerate fibers for the earliest papers. In the seventeenth century, a beater machine was invented in Holland, and variations of this machine are in use today. The beater macerates the fibers and pounds them with water until they are hydrocellulose—that is, until water has penetrated so deeply that many of the bonds between fibers are broken. Only then can the paper be made.

A sheet of paper is formed when a thin layer of these hydrocellulose fibers is lifted from the water on a sieve-like screen. The water drains, leaving a sheet of matted fibers some four or five times as thick as the final dried sheet will be.

Why Do Paper Fibers Stick Together?

During drying, fibers are drawn closer and closer together until, as the last of the water is dried out, surface tension causes hydrogen bonding to join adjacent cellulose molecules. No adhesives are necessary.

What Makes Handmade Paper Different?

Machine-made paper is fine for many uses; it can be produced quickly, efficiently, economically, and with regularity and precision. Today one machine averages a 200,000-pound roll of paper each day; a good papermaker can produce about 200 pounds of paper by hand in the same time.

But when you lavish effort on what you put on a sheet of paper, it makes sense to lavish some attention on what has gone into that paper as well. For many special uses, handmade paper can't be bettered. It is almost always 100 percent rag, so it is more durable than machine-made paper that does not have a rag-pulp base. It is made without chemicals or acid sizings that might shorten the life of the paper, and it is usually air-dried. Because handmade paper is produced one sheet at a time, it can be shaken in two directions as it drains to add strength; machine-made paper is vibrated in only one direction, and it is dried by passing it between hot rollers.

If you would like to read more about papermaking, ask your librarian for books by the late Dard Hunter, an authority on handmade paper. The Rare Books Room at your public or university library may have books printed on handmade paper.

How Is Paper Made At Twinrocker?

Opposite, two papermakers and an apprentice at the Twinrocker workshop in Brookston, Indiana, demonstrate the basic steps of making rag paper by hand. Following that are two projects—one for recycling paper with a blender, and one for making rag paper from prepared pulp.

How rag paper is made by hand at the Twinrocker workshop

This large beater, designed and built by Howard Clark, can turn three pounds of dry white cotton rags into pulp in about two hours. Such a machine is essential in making rag paper, but home craftsmen can buy prepared pulp.

Papermaker Timothy Barrett places the deckle (a wooden frame) atop the mould, a screen of brass wires that catch the paper fibers. Wire watermark shapes are attached. The deckle serves as a stencil in shaping the finished paper sheet.

Tim dips mould and deckle into a vat of pulp. He wears a rubber apron and boots to keep dry and ties a bandanna around his head to keep hair from falling onto the paper. The large, deep vat is made of wood coated with plastic resin.

After submerging the mould and deckle, he brings them to the surface to catch an even layer of fibers. For an extra large mould, two papermakers work together. It takes only seconds for a sheet of paper to be formed.

As excess water drains away, the papermaker shakes the mould to lessen the grain and help unite the fibers. In the photograph, the surface of the paper has already changed from shiny to dull; this means the fibers have set.

The mould is set on the side of the vat and the deckle is removed. Then the papermaker inspects the surface of the sheet carefully and removes any foreign particles or lumps of fibers with tweezers.

Tim and apprentice Lee McDonald work together to couch a new sheet of paper—that is, to transfer the paper from the mould onto a clean, damp felt for pressing.

The newly formed sheets of paper and the rectangular felts are alternately stacked in preparation for the pressing process. This procedure is called pulling the post, the post being a stack of sheets.

Papermaker Katherine Kiddie operates the workshop's 50-ton press; the smoothness of the paper depends on the amount of pressure applied. The felts are removed and the sheets of paper are air-dried, then stacked and pressed again.

These blender-made papers have been recycled, mostly from wood-pulp papers found around the house. To get color, start with colored paper or add liquid fabric dye.

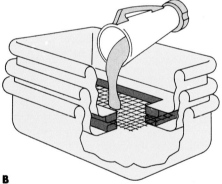

B
Figure B: When you recycle paper with a blender, the liquified pulp is poured into what is called a sheetmaker, shown here in a cut-away drawing. It is made of three plastic dishpans, aluminum screen and wood strips.

1: To make the top unit of a sheetmaker (see Figure B, above), mark a 5½-by-7½-inch rectangle on the bottom of a standard-size plastic dishpan and cut it out with a craft knife.

Environmental Projects
Blender-recycled paper   ¢ ◻ ⚼ 🔥

Machine-made papers that are readily available around the house, mostly made of wood pulp, can easily be recycled with the aid of a food blender. Newsprint, old homework papers, junk mail, paper towels, cereal and film boxes, magazine pages and used typing paper, can be converted into informal note paper or papers for other craft projects. Some used stationery, especially that bearing a letterhead, will be made of rag or partly-rag pulp. It, too, can be recycled.

The waste paper is first reduced to its original fibers and thoroughly mixed with water in a blender. Then it is restructured into a new sheet of paper. All wood-pulp papers are chemically treated during the manufacturing process, so you may find that some of your new paper will have spots of unexpected color. The paper might even cause stains when it is wet. This is not a problem in most cases, however. When you use paper that was printed with colored inks, such as the comic strips from the Sunday paper, the overall color of the new paper will be unpredictable—and that is part of the fun. Black-and-white newsprint will produce some tone of gray, depending on the amount of ink.

When you select the scrap papers for this project, pick out and discard any cellophane windows from envelopes, staples, tape or plastic pieces. Avoid brown paper bags or heavily coated magazine covers; they are very strong and are hard to break down in a blender. To make colored paper, start with colored stock or simply pour liquid fabric dye into the pulp in the blender until it is the color you want (vivid tints work best). Fabric dyes work well because cotton fabric and paper are chemically identical. The dye may fade in strong light, but this type of homemade paper is not intended to last forever. If you like, you can tint paper by brushing diluted dye onto damp sheets to achieve a soft watercolor effect.

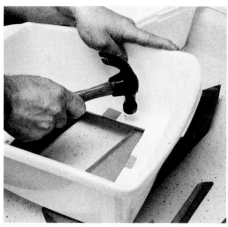

2: The deckle, which serves as a stencil in determining the size of the sheet of paper that will result, is made of four wooden strips cut to fit around the edges of the cut-out rectangle. A picture frame flat on both sides could be used.

3: Hold the wood strips on the bottom of the top dishpan with masking tape as you tack them on with ½-inch aluminum (non-rusting) tacks. Two tacks to a strip should be sufficient. Pound the tips flat on the other side.

4: Set the second dishpan inside the first, invert them, and trace the opening, using the deckle frame as a guide. Cut this rectangle out of the second dishpan. The third (bottom) dishpan is left uncut, to hold water and catch the overflow.

Materials and Tools

Set up your papermaking operation near the kitchen or laundry sink where running water is handy and cleanup will be easy. To assemble a sheetmaker that will make 5½- by 7½-inch sheets, you will need: three standard size kitchen dishpans made of plastic; about 5 feet of wood moulding strips, ¼ inch thick and ¾ inch wide; two or more pieces of aluminum window screening, each about 8 by 12 inches; ½-inch aluminum tacks; cloth or masking tape; a hammer; a craft knife; and a waterproof-ink marker. To make the paper you will also need: a heavy glass jar or rolling pin; a food blender; an iron; a chopping board to iron on (or other surface that can withstand stains and heat); a terrycloth towel; several cotton press cloths about 10 by 15 inches (pieces of an old sheet will do); and the papers you want to recycle.

The Sheetmaker

Three plastic dishpans are stacked to make the sheetmaker. The bottom dishpan holds water and catches the overflow that would otherwise go down the kitchen drain. The other two dishpans have identical rectangles cut out of their bottoms. These cutouts are framed with wood strips that form a deckle (essentially a stencil) to determine the size and shape of your new paper sheets. The deckle is attached to the bottom of the top dishpan, and to the top of the middle one (Figure B).

On the bottom of the top dishpan, outline a rectangle 5½ by 7½ inches, and cut it out with a craft knife (photograph 1).

Cut four wood strips to frame the rectangle (photograph 2). The corners can be mitered or butted, just as long as they meet snugly and form rectangles. You can use a ready-made picture frame if it is flat on both sides.

With masking or cloth tape, temporarily tape the strips to the outside bottom of the top dishpan. From the inside, tack the strips in place with ½-inch aluminum tacks—two into each strip will be sufficient (photograph 3). Do not use staples or steel nails or tacks because they would rust. Pound the projecting tips of the tacks flat, remove the tape, and trim any uneven edges on the plastic.

Next, turn the middle dishpan upside down and stack the top dishpan over it so you can trace the cutout on the bottom of the middle dishpan (photograph 4). Again, cut out the rectangle with a craft knife. Tape the wood strips in place, to the inside bottom of this dishpan (photograph 5), and tack them in position.

Next, layer the three dishpans in the proper order with a sheet of aluminum window screening between the top and middle tubs (photograph 6 and Figure B). The screen is not attached, but it should be large enough to extend beyond the edges of the opening so it will not buckle when the liquid pulp is poured through it. If you prefer a finer texture, try using two pieces of screening. Experiment a little—the number of screens will depend on the type of paper you start with and the kind of paper you want to make.

5: Four more wood deckle strips are taped, then tacked to the middle dishpan, this time to the inside. When the top dishpan with the outside deckle is set inside this one, the deckles will meet.

6: Put one or two pieces of aluminum window screen between the top and middle dishpans; then set both in the bottom one. The screen is not attached, but extends well beyond the deckle to prevent buckling.

7: Fill a blender three-quarters full with warm water and add small pieces of scrap paper, one at a time, until the liquid is cloudy but not thick. The blender speed to use will be determined by the weight of the paper. Approximately one full-size sheet of newspaper or two sheets of paper toweling are needed for one new sheet.

8: Put the sheetmaker in the kitchen sink and fill it with warm water just to the level of the screen. Pour the liquified pulp smoothly and evenly over the entire surface of the screen.

9: Lift the top two dishpans straight up and shake them gently from side to side and from front to back until the surface of the new paper turns from shiny to dull, which takes only seconds.

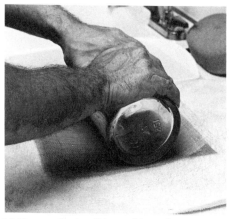

10: Remove the top dishpan, lift out the screen and lay it paper-side-up on a towel. Put another piece of screen on top and roll out excess moisture with a heavy glass jar or rolling pin.

11: The next step, called couching, is the transferring of the still-wet paper sheet from the screen to the "felt"—in this case a cotton press cloth on a wooden cutting board.

The Paper

Start by tearing up the scrap papers into small bits. At first, use just one type of paper at a time; later you can try combinations. If the paper you are using is stiff or heavy, such as cereal or film boxes, soak the pieces in hot water until they are soft before you add them to the blender. To make one sheet of recycled paper, you will need approximately one page of a full-size newspaper (two tabloid pages) or two sheets of paper toweling. Newspapers and tissue make soft papers; paper towels and boxes make stiff papers. The more paper you put in the blender, the thicker your new paper will be, but note that you need surprisingly little paper in the mix. The blender pulp should be very dilute and easy to pour, not thick and lumpy.

Fill the blender about three-quarters full with warm water. The speed you use for blending will depend on the weight of the paper, but generally you should start slowly, then advance the speed as the paper breaks down. Do not remove the lid from the blender while it is working; remove the center cap only or turn the blender off each time you add a new scrap of paper. Add the scraps one at a time, and let each piece break down completely before you add the next piece (photograph 7). The water will look a little foamy as it blends. If you use liquid dye, add it after all the paper pieces have been broken down.

When you have added all the paper, let the liquid pulp blend a bit longer while you set the three stacked dishpans in the sink and fill them with warm water just up to the level of the screen. Pour the liquid pulp from the blender slowly into the pans, distributing it evenly over the surface of the screen rather than pouring it all straight into the center (photograph 8 above, and Figure B, page 1390).

When all the pulp has been poured into the sheetmaker, hold the top and middle dishpans tightly together and lift them straight up and out of the bottom dishpan (photograph 9). This lets the water drain down through the screen and forces the pulp fibers to collect on top of the screen. Some fibers will escape between the deckle wood strips on the top and middle dishpans. This deckle edge is a sign that the paper has been made by hand.

Lift the dishpans quickly and smoothly, without tilting, shaking them gently from side to side and from front to back. There is a certain rhythm to this that takes practice. This two-way shaking unites the fibers even more and eliminates to some extent the grain of the paper, making it stronger and smoother. There will be a noticeable change on the surface of the paper sheet as its sets; when it turns from shiny to dull you should stop shaking (photograph 9).

Now you can lift off the top dishpan, revealing the newly-formed sheet on the screen. Lift the screen out, holding it by two diagonally opposite corners, and lay it on a terrycloth towel with the paper side up. Put a second piece of screen over the paper (use the bottom piece if you had two pieces in the sheetmaker), and roll out much of the excess water by going over this screen-and-paper sandwich with a heavy glass jar or rolling pin (photograph 10). Do this with a smooth even movement to avoid wrinkling the still-wet paper.

When much of the water has been pressed out, lift off the top screen and turn the bottom screen, paper side down, onto an ironing surface covered with a lint-free cotton press cloth. Do this with a rolling motion from one side to the other (photograph 11). This step is called couching (cooch-ing) from the French word *coucher* which means to lie down between blankets.

12: Put a second cotton cloth over the paper sheet and press with a warm, dry iron (you will be making your own steam). Keep the iron moving; move the paper occasionally to prevent sticking.

13: To add decorative interest, you can add thin, small things such as leaves, flower petals, bits of thread, feathers or blades of grass to the wet paper sheet before it is pressed.

14: You also can laminate two sheets of paper together for a two-toned effect, couching the second sheet from the screen directly onto the first while both are still very wet, then ironing.

You could let the paper sheet air dry, but you will probably want to speed things up at this point. You can help the paper dry by ironing it. Put a second cotton cloth over the paper sheet and press it with a warm, dry iron. Keep the iron moving; don't stop at any one place (photograph 12). Lift a corner of the press cloth and take a peek; when the paper seems to be getting dry, move it to another area of the press cloth or onto another cloth to keep it from sticking. Cotton is the best press cloth because it is the most absorbent. Your press cloth should not have a marked texture unless you want that texture impressed on your finished sheet. When the paper is nearly dry, you can iron it directly without using the press cloth. (If the paper starts to stick to the iron, however, it is not dry enough.)

You can embed things in your new sheet of paper while it is still wet and on the screen (photograph 13). A leaf, snips of thread, a feather, flower petals or blades of grass can be decorative. If the object is thick enough to make a bump, you may want to try laminating it between the first sheet and a second, thinner sheet. You can also laminate two sheets of different colors to get a two-toned effect. Photograph 14 shows a small sheet of yellow paper (liquid dyed) being laminated to a larger sheet of gray. If you laminate two sheets of equal size this way and fold them in half when dry, you will have note cards that are gray outside and yellow inside.

Handmade rag paper

Once you have recycled some existing scrap paper as described on the previous pages, you may want to try making your own rag paper. The principle of papermaking is the same, but the equipment and techniques are somewhat different.

The Pulp

First of all, you won't be using your own rags. Making rag pulp would be extremely difficult, if not impossible, without a beater machine. So you buy ready-made rag pulp. It is available by mail-order from these sources:

Twinrocker Handmade Paper, Brookston, Indiana 47923; The Craftool Co., Inc., 1421 West 240th Street, Harbor City, California 90710; and to schools only—Brodhead-Garrett Co., 4560 East 71st Street, Cleveland, Ohio 44105.

Write first to get current prices and quantities available. Pulp can be frozen and used a little at a time, or it can be shared with friends.

You will mix the pulp with warm water to make stock. For this, you need a large (about 36-gallon) plastic or galvanized metal tub, a stationary laundry tub, or a deep homemade plywood vat sealed with a plastic resin. Whatever you use, it should be 15 to 18 inches deep and have straight, not sloping, sides.

Tradition dictates that this poem by an unknown eighteenth-century author be included in any writings about handmade rag paper:

Rags make paper,
Paper makes money,
Money makes banks,
Banks make loans,
Loans make beggars,
Beggars make
            Rags.

Handmade paper with a 100 percent rag content deserves your best words (page 1386) or your best prints or artwork. The engraving on this 8½-by-11 inch sheet of paper depicts papermaking in an earlier era in Europe. Check antique shops or small newspapers or printers for engravings, or print your own woodcuts, block prints or silk screen designs.

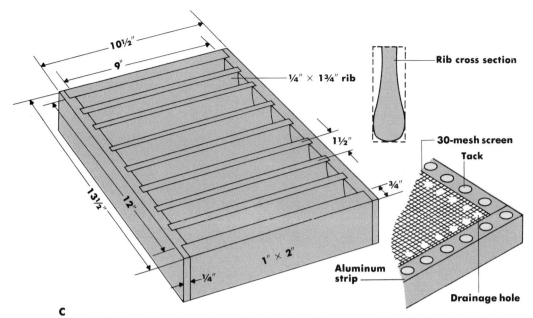

Labels on Figure C: 10½", 9", ¼" × 1¾" rib, Rib cross section, 1½", 13½", 12", ¾", 30-mesh screen, Tack, Aluminum strip, 1" × 2", ¼", Drainage hole

C

Figure C: This mould (used with the deckle below in making rag paper) is made of wood and aluminum screen. The tapered ribs beneath the screen detailed at the right are designed to create a greater suction as the paper fibers are lifted from the water suspension, and to support the screen under pressure.

This redwood deckle fits over a mould with a laid-and-chain screen of brass wires.

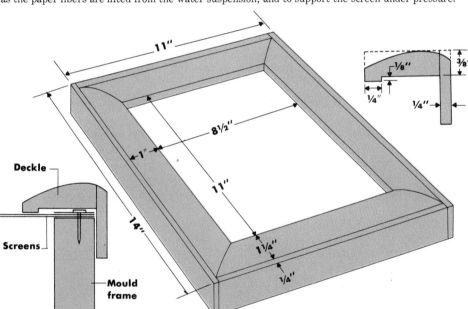

Labels on Figure D: 11", ⅛", ⅜", ¼", 8½", Deckle, 1", 11", Screens, 14", Mould frame, 1¼", ¼"

D

Figure D: This wood deckle, shaped like a picture frame, is placed over the ribbed mould in Figure C to shape the paper sheet by limiting the flow of pulp. This size makes a sheet of paper 8½ by 11 inches.

The Mould and the Deckle

To make rag paper, instead of pouring the liquid pulp through the sheetmaker as with blender-made paper, you dip the entire mould and deckle into the vat of stock. Diagrams showing a mould and deckle for an 8½ by 11 inch sheet are in Figures C and D. However, moulds and deckles can also be purchased from the Craftool Co. (address above). If you are a skilled woodworker, you may want to make your own; the tapered ribs shown in detail can be cut with a table saw and shaped with a rasp, or you can leave the ribs straight. Redwood or Honduras mahogany are the best woods because they contain oils that make them naturally rot resistant, but you can also use pine if you finish it carefully. Glue all joints with a powdered waterproof glue or a marine-grade plastic resin glue. Finish with four coats of urethane varnish, letting each coat dry thoroughly before applying the next. Precision shaping of the parts is very important; a mould and deckle assembly that is tight, strong and squared-off will last indefinitely.

A backview of the mould shows the shaped supporting ribs that hold the screen rigid and aid drainage by creating a suction.

This mould, with a wire watermark attached, has two layers of aluminum screen. The small holes punched around the inner edges of the screen are there to speed drainage.

The two sizes of screen can be discerned in this close-up picture of the mould above. Although the watermark used on Twinrocker papers is intricate, the shaped wire does not overlap.

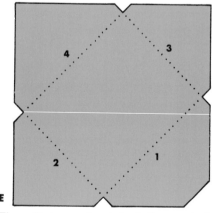

Figure E: An envelope is basically a notched square, with one corner cut off. Dotted lines indicate folds. Sealing wax is the finishing touch (see photograph on page 1386).

Cover the top side of the mould with 4-mesh-to-the-inch aluminum screening. Brass, stainless steel, or other non-corroding screen can also be used, but aluminum is the most readily available. Tack the edges down with aluminum tacks. Then cover this large-mesh screen with a smaller mesh (30-mesh-to-the-inch if available) for a finely textured paper. Hold the edges with aluminum strips and tacks. Punch small drainage holes around the screen edges, ¼ inch apart. This type of mould is called a wove mould because of the woven texture of the screen. The texture is almost invisible on the finished sheet, however, making the paper ideal for art purposes because there is no surface texture to interfere with color washes or subtle shadings. The earliest mould surfaces were made from strips of bamboo laid side by side to make a screen. Traditional European moulds were similar, but brass wires were used instead of bamboo. Called a laid or laid-and-chain mould, this type produces a definite texture on the paper that is preferred by book printers. This type of mould would be very difficult to make by hand, however. An example of paper made on such a mould is shown in the photograph below, left.

The removable deckle on top of the mould is the stencil that gives the paper sheet its shape. A machine-made deckle edge is an imitation of the uneven edge that results on handmade paper when stray fibers escape underneath a deckle. This uneven edge makes extra care necessary in centering a print. An envelope shape is basically a notched square with one corner cut off (see Figure E). Fold the corners inward on the dotted lines in sequence as numbered. The last triangle is the envelope flap.

The sun god is an example of a continuous-tone watermark made by molding the surface screen into highs and lows. The background shows the pattern of a laid mould made of brass wires.

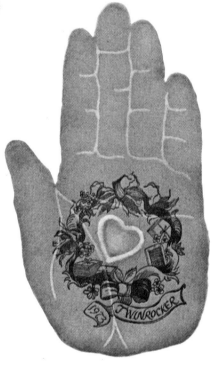

This heart-in-hand design, a combination of watermarks and printing on paper made in the hand shape, was the Twinrocker Christmas card in 1973.

Watermarks

A watermark is an impressive addition to your stationery, but you do not make a watermark with water. The usual watermark results when thin (.030 inch) copper wire is bent into a flat shape, then is fastened with nylon thread to the top of the mould screen. When the mould is lifted up through the pulp and shaken, fewer fibers collect where the wire is, causing a thinner and thereby somewhat translucent pattern there. In machine-made paper, fibers are displaced while the sheet is still wet by rolling the watermark over the sheet. Watermarks show best when they are held up to the light, and they are most noticeable on thin papers.

When you make your watermark shape, take care not to overlap the wire at any point. This would cause the wires to be too thick at that spot—they could tear through the paper. As an example, Figure F shows how the small letter "t" might be formed without overlap. Use as few wires as possible in the design, but the design doesn't need to be small; it can fit in one corner or cover the entire sheet. A watermark pattern can also be formed by molding the wires of the mould screen, but this technique is usually complicated and rarely used in the United States. This intricate process creates a watermark with continuous tones, rather than sharp lines, such as the watermark portraits often seen on European currency. The sun in the photograph on the opposite page was created this way.

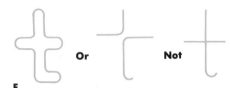

F
Figure F: Overlapped wires in a watermark (right) can make the shape tear the wet paper. Instead of crossing wires, bend them so all elements are on one plane (left and center).

The Paper Itself

To make rag paper, fill the vat with warm water and add the pulp, thoroughly mixing the two. This is called charging the vat. Add about one gallon of pulp to every 30 gallons of water. This is only an estimate; the first sheet will show you by its thickness and evenness if the proportion should be changed. You can also add snips of thread, feathers, flower petals and the like for a surprise in each sheet.

When the deckle is not in use, it can float on the surface of the stock and you can use it to stir the mixture occasionally (photograph 15). Be sure to stir the stock before making each sheet. Do not do this with the mould, however; fibers would stick to the underside of the screen and spoil future sheets.

The motion of dipping the mould and deckle into the vat and out is a smooth, rhythmic one that takes practice. First, lean out over the vat with the mould and deckle held firmly together at the short sides (one long side should be on top). Dip the mould straight down, parallel to the back of the vat (photograph 16). When the mould is almost completely submerged, start to scoop it forward (photograph 17). By the time the mould is completely submerged, it should be horizontal, parallel to the bottom of the vat. Now bring it straight up and out of the stock (photograph 18), draining the water and creating a suction that brings the paper fibers together. Gently shake the mould from side to side and then from front to back, keeping it as horizontal as you can without tilting it. This shaking motion sets the fibers and diminishes the grain. (Machine-made paper in a roll can be agitated in only one direction, so it retains more grain than handmade paper.) These steps should follow without a break, and your hands should never leave the mould.

15: The first step in making rag paper is called charging the vat—thoroughly mixing the liquid rag pulp with warm water. The deckle, but never the mould, is used to stir the milky white stock.

16: Dipping the mould and deckle in one smooth, scooping motion takes practice. Hold the mould and deckle firmly together, long sides top and bottom, and start in the middle of the vat with the mould perpendicular to the bottom.

17: Slide the mould and deckle straight down into the pulp until they are almost submerged. Then start to scoop them forward as well. When submerged, they should be horizontal, parallel to the bottom of the vat.

18: Now bring the mould and deckle straight up and out of the vat, draining the water and creating a suction that unites the fibers. Gently, but quickly, shake the mould in both directions. Be sure to keep it level.

19: Set the mould on the side of the vat so that it will continue to drain, and lift off the deckle, exposing the edges of the newly-formed sheet of paper. The deckle can float on the surface of the liquid in the vat until you are ready to use it for the next sheet.

20: Taking the wet paper off the mould (called couching) is also done with one continuous motion that takes practice. Turn the mould paper side down (it won't fall off), and rest one edge of the mould on a piece of old blanket or similar material (called the felt). The felt should be damp.

21: Lay the mould down, being sure that all edges of the paper sheet are on the felt, and press with both hands. Because the wet paper has a greater affinity for the damp felt, it will stick to the felt and come away from the screen of the mould.

22: With a single smooth rolling motion, lift the mould from the paper. Notice that the first edge to be set down is the first edge to be lifted. Do not rock the mould back and forth over the wet sheet—this causes wrinkles.

23: Because its water content is high, this new sheet is thicker than it will be when it is dry. Stray fibers around the edges make the deckle edge; the cause-and-effect of the watermark is obvious.

Now set the mould on the side of the vat to drain more. Remove the deckle, and let it float in the vat until you are ready to make another sheet (photograph 19). Inspect the paper on the mould; use tweezers gingerly to remove any foreign particles from the surface. If you have made a bad sheet (one that is uneven or has holes), you can turn the mould face down on the surface of the vat liquid, peel or knock the sheet off, and stir the wet fibers immediately back into the stock.

The next step is called couching. Here, the sheet is transferred from the mould to a flat surface such as a plywood board mounted about 18 inches off the floor. (Later, this board will become the bottom press board.) Cover this board with several damp felts for padding. Pieces of old blankets are ideal felts, but you can use any loosely woven, woolen fabric that has a slightly rough texture and does not lint. Felts must be washed and pressed frequently so they are clean and lint-free. Cut them about 4 inches larger in all directions than your paper sheets. After the first sheet, only one felt is needed between sheets. All the felts should be damp.

To couch the paper sheet onto a felt, turn the mould over, paper side down. It won't fall off because it is still wet enough to stick to the screen. Because it has more of an affinity for the felt, however, it will readily come off the screen and stick to the felt. Set one edge of the mould at the edge of the felt, being sure to center the sheet of paper (photograph 20). Then, with a rolling motion, lower the mould onto the felt and press as hard as you can (photograph 21). Lift the mould back up, with the far edge the last to leave the felt (photograph 22). Like dipping into the vat, couching is one smooth, quick, continuous motion that requires practice. Don't rock the mould; this will cause wrinkles. (The mould shown in photograph 22 is a laid mould—notice the fine wires showing between the ribs.) When the mould is lifted from the felt, the sheet stays behind (photograph 23).

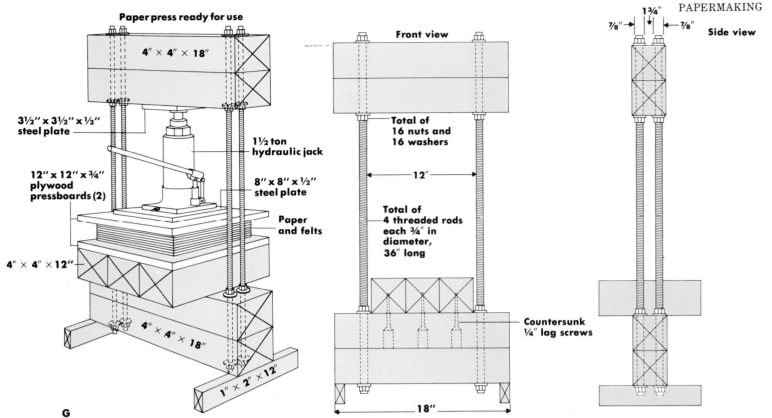

Paper press ready for use

4″ × 4″ × 18″

3½″ x 3½″ x ½″ steel plate

12″ × 12″ × ¾″ plywood pressboards (2)

1½ ton hydraulic jack

8″ × 8″ × ½″ steel plate

Paper and felts

4″ × 4″ × 12″

4″ × 4″ × 18″

1″ × 2″ × 12″

Front view

Total of 16 nuts and 16 washers

12″

Total of 4 threaded rods each ¾″ in diameter, 36″ long

Countersunk ¼″ lag screws

18″

Side view

7/8″   1 3/4″   7/8″

G

Figure G: You can build your own paper press with a 1½-ton hydraulic jack. Use solid, dense lumber (oak or Douglas fir), and coat everything with urethane varnish. After the paper is couched onto the lower press board, put the second press board on top and place the pack in the press. Center the larger steel plate on the top board, center the jack on that plate, and center the smaller steel plate on top of the jack. By operating the jack, you will press out the excess water in the paper.

We call layering a stack of sheets between felts *pulling a post*. Do not stack more than 70 sheets at one time—the weight of the paper, felts, board and water will be more than you expect.

Finally, you will press the entire stack. If you do not have access to a book binder's standing press, you can build your own (see Figure G, above).

After pressing, the sheets will still be wet, but not so wet they cannot be separated from the felts and dried individually. Air drying is another treatment given only to handmade paper (machine-made paper is dried between hot rollers). Gently lift each sheet from the felt onto a clean screen and give it time to dry naturally. You can use a silk-screen drying rack or fashion a rack from pieces of window screen stacked between bricks or boards (Figure H) or bridged between two chair seats and weighted down at the sides. When the sheets are almost dry, they can be stacked again, without any felts this time, and pressed once more. The more you press, the smoother the surfaces of the sheets will be.

Only the Beginning

Of course, making the paper is only a first step. No matter how beautiful, it is incomplete without something on it—a poem, a woodcut print, an invitation lettered in calligraphy, a charcoal sketch, the beginning of a novel.

Because the paper is unsized (that is, without a finish), it should be printed dry. You can write on it with a typewriter, ballpoint pen or felt-tipped marker; draw on it with pencil, charcoal, crayon or chalk. If you write with ink and a fountain or quill pen, you will find the ink is quickly absorbed and spreads out over the surface of the paper. To prevent this, you can spray both sides of the sheet with a clear acrylic coating; let it dry thoroughly before writing. This will only slightly alter the texture and feel of the paper.

For related entries and crafts, see "Airplanes of Paper," "Block Printing," "Bookbinding," "Calligraphy," "Greeting Cards;" "Linoleum and Woodcuts," "Monoprinting," "Quill Pens," "Serigraphy" and "Valentines."

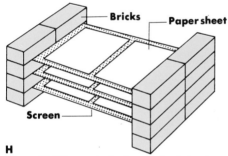

Bricks

Paper sheet

Screen

H

Figure H: When a stack of paper sheets has been made and pressed (Figure G), they are laid out separately on a screen so air can circulate around to dry them. Pieces of screen stacked between bricks serve the purpose well.

If you do silk screening, you may have a drying rack such as this available. It is helpful if you are making large quantities of paper.

PAPIER-MÂCHÉ
Old News Is Good News

With a little wallpaper paste, a dab of paint, and a few other household odds and ends, you can turn yesterday's newspapers into colorful characters like those pictured opposite and on the pages that follow—bottle people, a witch, a cowboy and a gentle monster. Papier-mâché, a material made of nothing but paper and paste, has been used for centuries. The Chinese probably invented it, but Japanese and Persian craftsmen were not far behind in being among the first to employ it. By the seventeenth century, it was being used in Europe to make boxes, trays, and even furniture such as tables and chairs. The name comes from the French language and means "chewed-up paper." It is said that French women were once employed to chew paper into pulp to prepare it for sculpting.

Advantages

Papier-mâché has retained its popularity through the centuries with both craftsmen and artists. The basic materials—scrap paper and paste—are inexpensive and readily available. Because they are natural and biodegradable, the cleanup is easy. No chemical solvents or special tools are needed. Best of all, papier-mâché has great possibilities. Like clay, it is pliable and responsive to the touch, and permanent sculptured forms can be achieved without the use of a kiln (all you need to harden papier-mâché is air). You can leave the finished form to dry to its natural, rough-textured state, or you can smooth the surface with sandpaper or a file after the sculpture has dried. Papier-mâché provides a natural surface for collage, and bits of many types of paper (for instance colored tissue paper, construction paper, fancy wrapping paper, stamps, and motifs clipped from flower catalogs or greeting cards) can be glued onto the finished sculpture. Many other materials may be used for surface decoration, including paint, string, beads, yarn, sequins, ribbon, fabric scraps, and odds and ends of wood, plastic and glass. Best of all the craft can be as simple or elegant as you want to make it. And it is just messy enough, in a harmless way, to delight children.

One characteristic of papier-mâché that takes some getting used to is the tendency of the material to shrink as it dries. This may be overcome by making the wet model larger than you want the finished size to be. But even with a dried and shrunken model, you can always wet the surface and add new layers of papier-mâché until the desired size and appearance are achieved. A third course, one I often take, is simply to relax and see what happens. Shrinkage can be annoying, but it also can add to the fun. I am often pleasantly surprised by the personality a somewhat shriveled face imparts to one of my characters.

The Armature

Structures made of papier-mâché need some sort of support in much the same way the human body needs a skeleton. When the support actually resembles a skeleton, as in the bent wire frame inside the dinosaur figure on page 1407 it is called an armature. In addition to wire, a supporting frame can be made of wood, wadded-up paper, clay or glass. It may be permanent or temporary, as demonstrated by the two methods of making a puppet head shown on page 1406. Parts of the support may even remain visible and become a part of the finished design, as in the bottle people pictured opposite. Although you could build up a form using only papier-mâché, a support of some sort will save time and material, allow more design freedom, and add strength to the final product.

Trudy Feiss is a sculptress who works almost exclusively in "city clay"—her name for papier-mâché. Her travels throughout the United States have allowed her to study painting, sculpture and design at several different schools and to exhibit her work at many galleries and shows. As a teacher, she has brought craft skills to many children and adults.

Papier-mâché, long associated with the cute and colorful, assumes a new potential in the hands of a serious sculptor. Shown here is "The Taxpayer," a sculpture by Trudy Feiss. The artist covered a wire armature with layers of hardware cloth, papier-mâché pulp and strips to build up the figure. A final layer of torn-up income tax forms suggests the clothing—and the possibility of relating papier-mâché to the artist's subject. The careful selection of props (such as the "HELP" rubber stamp) and a minimal application of paint are characteristic of Ms. Feiss's work.

Most people casually dispose of bottles—once they have served their function as containers—without giving them a second thought. But Trudy Feiss, an energetic recyclist with the gift of seeing potential in everyday objects, salvages bottles and transforms them into delightful bottle people such as the two shown opposite, a fringed fellow on the left and Mrs. Calabash on the right. The next time you empty a ketchup bottle or a pickle jar, take a good look; there may be a bottled-up personality lurking there, just waiting for you to free him. Directions begin on page 1403.

CRAFTNOTES: PAPIER-MÂCHÉ STRIPS AND PULP

Each of the two types of papier-mâché used today, strips and pulp (or mash), has its own characteristics, but the two forms are compatible and can be combined so you have the advantages of both. The strip method is a very direct and straightforward technique, and can be used to build up thick surfaces quickly. Papier-mâché pulp takes longer to prepare, but because the paper fibers have been loosened, it can be used to form delicate shapes, and the surface can be made textured or smooth, just as with modeling clay.

Papier-mâché pulp can be made at home or purchased at craft stores and hobby shops. Commercial pulp is convenient for small projects, but because both shrinkage and cost are high, it is not recommended for large ones. Wheat paste powder for the paste solution is sold in craft shops and hardware stores, where it is sometimes called wallpaper paste. You may find that you'd like to add a squirt of white household glue to the paste solution, or even substitute white glue diluted with water for the wheat paste. Newsprint is commonly used in papier-mâché today, but you may want to experiment with paper toweling, facial tissue, gift wrap, wrapping paper, discarded envelopes, or even old brochures. When making papier-mâché pulp, avoid using heavy brown wrapping paper or any glossy paper that has a coating on it. The fibers in these papers are very difficult to separate.

Strip Method
In the strip method, newsprint or other paper is torn into strips about ¾ inch wide; these are dipped into the paste solution, which should be made just prior to use. You will need: newspapers; wheat paste; water; a large container for mixing the paste; and a stirrer.
Begin by tearing the paper into strips. Tearing is better than cutting

because torn edges are softer and blend into each other more readily than do sharp cut edges. If it seems hard to tear even strips, you may be tearing against the grain—the direction paper fibers run. Try tearing in the other direction. Immerse the paper strips in a thin solution of wheat paste and water which has been mixed following the directions on the paste package (above). Place several strips of paper in the solution at once, and make sure they are thoroughly coated. If you are working with very heavy paper such as brown wrapping paper, soaking the strips in the paste for several minutes, or overnight, will make them easier to handle.

Remove the strips from the paste one at a time, and wipe off excess paste between two fingers (above). The strip is now ready to be applied to an armature or other support, or to be formed into whatever shape you need for your project.

Pulp
A good papier-mâché pulp requires cooking—and quite a lot of it. It takes seven or eight stove-top hours (depending on the type of paper) of simmering to separate the paper fibers and reduce them to a mash. If you have space, large batches can be prepared and stored in a refrigerator for future use. To make pulp you will need: newspaper; water; wheat paste; an old metal cooking pan (use one you won't mind being blackened by newspaper ink); a container for mixing wheat paste and water; a stirring implement; a strainer; and a container for mixing and storing the prepared pulp.

Begin by shredding newspaper into small squares. Place the torn paper in the cooking pot until it is three-quarters full; cover it with enough water so it can be stirred easily. Let the paper soak overnight. Then, cook the mixture over a low flame, stirring occasionally so the paper does not settle to the bottom. The paper will begin to disintegrate in six or seven hours. Cook the mixture for one more hour; then let it cool. Remove the excess moisture from the pulp by squeezing small quantities against the strainer. Spread the pulp out on several thicknesses of newspaper, and let it drain overnight.

The next morning, mix together wheat paste and water until it reaches the consistency of heavy cream. Then combine roughly one cup of this mixture with three cups of drained paper pulp. To do this, alternately put small amounts of paste and pulp into the storage container, stirring constantly. You should achieve a lump-free mixture that has no excess water and is slightly tacky to the touch.

Variations
To make a small amount of pulp without cooking, whir it in an electric blender, using plenty of water and putting only small amounts of paper in the blender at one time.

Various additives can be used. For instance, a sprinkling of whiting (sold at hardware stores) added to the pulp as a filler makes a whiter, denser mash. Linseed oil acts as an extender, making the mash easier to work with and giving the finished product extra toughness. If you like the scent, oil of cloves or oil of wintergreen acts as a preservative, preventing the mash from turning sour as it ages.

Storage
Papier-mâché pulp will tend to decay after a period of time. Store it in a tightly closed container in your refrigerator. Even without a preservative, it will stay fresh for several weeks.

Pulp or Strips

Papier-mâché can be either paper pulp or paper strips (see Craftnotes opposite). I use both, often in combination in the same sculpture. In the strip method, paper is torn into strips, then coated with a solution of paste and water. These can be applied over a supporting frame or formed into small shapes with the fingers. The strip method is often used when a textured surface is sought. Pulp, used for smoother surfaces and finer details, consists of paper whose fibers have been loosened and combined with paste and water to make a mash that resembles clay. Pulp can be modeled with fingers or tools; it can be squeezed, pinched, smoothed, or delicately manipulated. If you like, you can form a basic shape or cover a frame with strips, then apply pulp over this rough form to create details such as fingers, toes, ears, noses, chins, eyebrows and mouths.

Designs and Decorations
Bottle people ¢ ● 👯 🦉

You need just the right bottles to make bottle people like Mrs. Calabash and the fringed fellow pictured on page 1401. The personality of the figure is largely determined by the shape of the bottle. Obviously, you wouldn't be able to make a tall, elegant lady if you started with a short, dumpy bottle.

Children especially enjoy this kind of project, since they seem to be adept at bestowing compatible personalities on inanimate objects. Our friend wearing the fringe and holding the flowers was made using only papier-mâché in strip form; this method is the better one for children because the strips are easy for young fingers to manipulate. Mrs. Calabash was made with both strips and pulp papier-mâché. Pulp can be used successfully by older children who are capable of making such details as smooth noses and fingers.

Materials

Except for paint and paint brushes, which are found in art supply stores, most of the materials required for this project can be found around the house or in a variety store. In addition to the bottle, you will need: papier-mâché pulp and strips (Craftnote, opposite); poster or acrylic paint; large and small paintbrushes; white glue; scissors and sandpaper or a file (optional); cardboard; trims for costumes may be bits of ribbon, lace, netting, fabric, and artificial flowers; yarn, steel wool, wood shavings, or scouring pads may serve as hair.

Applying Papier-Mâché

After choosing a bottle you feel is appropriate, wash it inside and out, and, if necessary, soak it in hot water to remove the label. Cover all work surfaces with sheets of newspaper. Cover the floor, too, if young children are helping. I find that a layer of waxed paper over the newspapers keeps the papier-mâché from sticking. Prepare paper strips as described in the Craftnotes opposite. Then wrap the bottle with a layer of horizontal strips (photograph 1). To help prevent the paper strips from cracking, you can apply a second layer of vertical strips, but this is optional. When you reach the bottom of the bottle, use short, vertical strips that curl under the bottom edge, covering it.

Building Up the Features

You can use either pulp or paper strips to form details. If only a few bottle people are planned, making your own pulp is hardly worth the bother if you can buy it.

Heads, ears, noses and feet: Ropes made by twisting paper strips together (photograph 2) may be wrapped around the bottle to form a head (photograph 3). Use thinner, smaller twisted ropes to make the arms. To form the feet, nose or ears, crumple a soaked paper strip into a small wad and press it onto the surface. (The fringed fellow's features were made this way; after drying, he was ready for painting.) Mrs. Calabash, a smoother character, has a coat of pulp applied in small amounts (photograph 4). While it is wet, such a surface may be smoothed with a fingertip, shaped into features, or textured with a fork or a pencil.

1: To cover a bottle with papier-mâché, wrap strips around it, overlapping them about ¼ inch. Press each strip from the middle outward to force out air bubbles and excess paste.

2: Gently twist several soaked strips of newspaper together to make a long, thick rope that can be used for the head or arms.

3: To make the head of a bottle figure, wrap two or three ropes (depending on their length) around the bottle, pressing them down so they adhere.

4: Press small amounts of papier-mâché pulp onto the damp surface being covered. Build up the form gradually, working in thin layers. Here, the head of a bottle figure is being shaped.

1403

5: Hands can be decorative or designed to hold objects such as a flower. These belong to the fringed black-haired boy pictured on page 1401 and were made from small wads of paper strips. The space between hands and body is designed to hold the flower stem securely.

6: Papier-mâché bottle people are not very impressive before they are painted and dressed. The fringed fellow-to-be at the left has almost been brought to life with a few props, but Mrs. Calabash, whose hands will be added after she is painted, is still quite dull.

7: To make a papier-mâché hat, first cut a circle of cardboard (the bigger the circle, the wider the hat brim will be). Slash the center as you would section a pie. Try the hat on the bottleneck and lengthen the slashes if necessary. When you are ready to place the hat permanently, cover it with strips of paper. If the bottle is to hold a candle, protect the hat with aluminum foil.

Hands: If the hands of your figure will be holding something, such as the flowers or the purse shown in the examples pictured, it will take a bit of planning to determine when and how the hands should be formed. Design the hands with the object to be held in mind, making sure it will fit (photograph 5). The boy is holding a flower that can be removed, so his hands were formed at the same time as the rest of the figure, before he was painted. Mrs. Calabash, on the other hand, is clinging to her possessions for dear life. Her fingers are firmly curled around the flower stem and the handle of her purse. These objects are permanently attached and would have been in the way while she was being painted; so all the other features were formed and the body was dried and painted before the hands were formed (photograph 6). Then hands were designed around the objects they are holding and were allowed to dry, then painted.

Be sure to let the papier-mâché dry thoroughly. This may take only overnight or several days, depending on the thickness of the material and the drying conditions. In the Craftnotes on the opposite page, ways are suggested to reduce the drying time. The shrinkage of the papier-mâché, especially if it is the pulp form, may alter your sculpture to such a degree that you will barely be able to recognize it. If the shrinkage destroys your concept, wet the surface and fill shrunken spots with more papier-mâché—you can add indefinitely—until you are satisfied with the results. Let each layer of added-on papier-mâché dry. When you are finished, you can smooth the surface with sandpaper or a file if you like.

Painting and Decorating

At this stage, your bottle people will look awkward, gray and lumpy (photograph 6). This is the time to liven things up by deciding how you will paint and decorate them. Gather scraps of fabric and other materials and spread them out. Pretend the figures are dolls and begin to dress them to see what works. Try on a ribbon bow tie or a fake flower corsage, some yarn for hair, a scrap of cloth for a skirt or a scarf. You may want to make a cardboard hat (photograph 7). Relax and enjoy this step; the most unlikely materials often work out beautifully. Mrs. Calabash's golden curls, for example, are made from a scouring pad fitted over the neck of the bottle.

When you have decided which materials you will use, paint the figure, applying as many coats of paint as necessary to cover it. You may decide to paint the entire figure, or to leave some areas unpainted. Because I like the juxtaposition of bright color with gray newsprint, I left some areas unpainted. My more serious sculptures are almost entirely unpainted (photograph, page 1400).

When the paint is dry, a protective coating of lacquer, varnish or clear acrylic will make the papier-mâché water-resistant and more durable.

At last, the dressing can begin. But first take a good look at what has evolved. Painting the figure may have changed its personality, and it may look better with a costume other than the one you originally chose. When you have decided what you want to do, use white household glue to hold hair, ribbons, and cloth in place. Mrs. Calabash's veil (cut from a net bag in which onions were packed) is tied around the neck of the bottle above the hat brim. The flower trim is tucked into the veil. The fringed fellow owes his fringe to a wig that is easy to make. Sew yarn onto a thin ribbon (Figure A); then glue the ribbon to the head. Wood shavings glued to the head make another interesting hair-do.

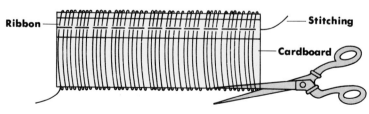

Ribbon — **Stitching**
Cardboard

A

Figure A: To make a yarn wig, start with a strip of cardboard as wide as the length of hair and long enough to encircle the head. Put a ¼-inch-wide ribbon along the length of the cardboard near the top edge, and hold the ends with tape. Wind yarn around the cardboard; tape the ends to the back. With thread, stitch the yarn to the ribbon, catching several wrappings (but not the cardboard) in each stitch; end with a knot. Cut the loops of yarn, loosen the tape, and slide the cardboard out of the yarn.

Toys and Games
Puppet heads

Bubble bubble, it's no toil or trouble to conjure up hand puppets like this witch, using papier-mâché over a dry newspaper or clay base. Directions for making such puppets begin below.

Of the many puppets I have made, these shown here are two of my favorites. In addition to general directions for puppet-making, specific directions for the cowboy and the witch are given. Before you begin, cover the work surface with newspapers and waxed paper.

Materials
To make a puppet head, you will need: papier-mâché in strip form (Craftnotes, page 1402); non-hardening modeling clay or dry newspaper for wadding; a craft knife or single-edged razor blade; masking tape; pencil; weighted jar or can; scissors; thin cardboard or posterboard; small brown paper bag (optional); sandpaper or file (optional); white glue or clear household cement; water-based paint such as poster paint or acrylic; paint brush; fabric scraps (if you use felt, you won't need to make hems because the edges won't ravel); and needle and thread. To make the cowboy you will also need: steel wool for eyebrows and moustache; rope or twine for the hatband; ruler; pencil; and paper for a pattern. For the witch, you will need steel wool for the hair and eyebrows, and a stick or twig.

Making a Puppet Head
Puppet heads are best made over a base; if you make them out of solid papier-mâché, they take too long to dry. I recommend the two methods described below, but you might like to try working on a partly inflated balloon. With a balloon, you

This old cowpoke named Steel-eyed Pete rolls up his sleeves to reveal a secret—his arms are the thumb and middle finger of the puppeteer; the forefinger maneuvers his papier-mâché head.

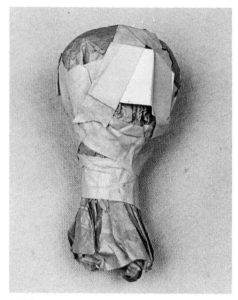

8: A brown paper bag filled with crumpled dry newspaper and shaped with masking tape makes a smooth-surfaced puppet-head base that can be left inside the head. Insert the cardboard neck and crimp the bag around it, fastening it with a piece of tape. Trim off any excess paper at the bottom. Here, to help in forming a prominent nose, a creased piece of cardboard was taped to the face.

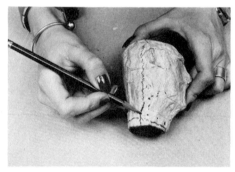

9: To make this puppet-head base, papier-mâché made of strips of paper toweling, rather than newspaper, were applied over a head formed from non-hardening modeling clay. Paper toweling is a bit more pliable than newspaper, and results in a smoother surface. If you use clay, after the papier-mâché dries, draw a guideline around the head; then slit the head into two sections with a craft knife or razor blade and remove the clay. Then tape the two halves together again.

get a nicely rounded shape, but wet balloons are slippery and hard to handle. Using a light bulb is difficult for children, since I have found it almost impossible to remove the light bulb without breaking it after the papier-mâché has dried.

While you work on a puppet head, painting or decorating it, you may find it a help to support the head with a pencil put into the neck and then into a jar or can weighted with clay or pebbles. I use this device to display the finished puppet.

Dry newspaper base: Working over a base of crumpled dry newspaper with a neck of cardboard is the simplest way to make a papier-mâché puppet head; it is also the best method for children to use. Crumple a sheet of newspaper into a ball slightly smaller than the head will be; wrap some masking tape around it. To make the neck, wrap a 2-inch-wide strip of thin cardboard loosely around your index finger several times, forming a tube; hold the end with tape. When you use the finished puppet, your index finger will be inserted into the neck to support and move the head; so be sure to leave enough room for a comfortable fit. If you wish, a small brown paper bag filled with crumpled newspaper can be used instead of the crumpled paper ball (photograph 8). Prepare paper strips (Craftnotes, page 1402) and cover the base with several layers of strips. Facial features may be shaped at this point (children will be anxious to see quick results), or the papier-mâché may be allowed to dry, then dampened slightly when features are added later. The papier-mâché will shrink; so the features will have to be reshaped in any event after they have dried.

Clay base: The use of a clay base is a good method for older children who have more patience and strive for greater perfection. The face and neck are first shaped in non-hardening modeling clay, which allows maximum flexibility. Keep the modeling simple; such details as ears and eyebrows should be added later. When the base is finished, cover it with at least six layers of paper strips. Use strips soaked only in water for the first layer, so they do not stick to the clay. Alternate the direction of the strips with each succeeding layer.

The costume may be glued on, but if you plan to sew it on for greater durability, pierce holes around the neck with an icepick before the papier-mâché dries. Then let the head dry and slit it in half so you can remove the clay (photograph 9). Tape the two halves together again and cover the seam with paper strips. At this point, you can add ears and improve the other features with more strips or pulp. Let the added material dry; then smooth the surface with a file or sandpaper if you like.

Painting and Decorating

Paint the head one color with one or two coats of paint, letting it dry between coats. Then add details such as the eyes and mouth. To make the hair, glue on yarn, steel wool, or whatever you like. Quick and easy is this method: put a coat of glue on the scalp area; then dip the head in wood shavings, dried tea leaves or coffee grounds and let the glue dry. Finally, improvise a costume from scraps of fabric, cardboard and yarn, using the costumes of the witch and cowboy for inspiration.

The Witch

I formed the witch's head over a clay base. Her unique and witch-like expression is accidental. I was so anxious to complete the puppet that I removed the clay before the papier-mâché was dry. The collapsed features resembled those of a witch, and I took advantage of this minor disaster by distorting them even more. In papier-mâché, as in many other crafts, accidents often trigger new design ideas.

Puppets don't always need hands of their own; in many cases the fingertips of the puppeteer serve well enough. In the case of the witch, however, hands add to her character. This is how to make them: wrap a thin piece of cardboard loosely around your middle finger and thumb (these are the fingers that will work the hands of the finished puppet; so be sure the fit is comfortable). Cut the cardboard about 1½ inches wide and long enough to wrap around the fingertips several times. Secure the end with tape. Using your own hands as the models, form hands and wrists over the cardboard tubes, using strips of papier-mâché. Here, the hand holding the stick is cup-shaped; the stick was attached with papier-mâché afterward.

As for the dressing and decorating, the hair and eyebrows are bits of steel wool attached with clear household cement (white glue doesn't hold metal).

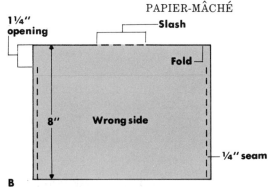

The gown is a 16-by-11-inch rectangle of black fabric folded in half crosswise and sewn together (Figure B). Insert the neck in the neck opening, and glue or sew the fabric to the neck. Then insert the wrists in the sleeve openings and glue the fabric to the papier-mâché. The head scarf is an 8-inch square of fabric folded into a triangle and tied under the puppet's chin. As a finishing touch, heavy black yarn was tied in a bow around the neck.

Steel-eyed Pete the Cowboy

To make Steel-eyed Pete, start by making a head over a base of dry newspaper, then paint it brown. Eyebrows and moustache are bits of steel wool held with clear household cement. Make his shirt from fabric measuring about 10 by 20 inches (Figure C). Insert the neck in the neck opening, and glue or sew it to the fabric. Make the bandana from a 6-inch square of bright fabric; fold it into a triangle and tie it around his neck. To make a hat from pieces of thin cardboard, cut as follows: for the brim, cut a circle about 5 inches in diameter; from the center, cut a circle large enough so the brim fits over the top of the puppet's head. Reserve the center circle to use as the top of the crown. For the crown, cut a 1¾-inch-wide piece of thin cardboard long enough to be wrapped around the head once, with a ½-inch overlap. Assemble the pieces as shown in Figure D. Paint the hat and trim it with a piece of twine. Put the completed hat on the puppet's head and glue it in place.

Designs and Decorations
The gentle monster

An armature made from soft wire and dry newspaper, used in the dinosaur model pictured below, can support almost any sort of figure you might want to make out of papier-mâché, from a mermaid to an elephant.

Marvelous monsters, both meek and mighty, can be made by using a wire armature as a skeleton to build upon. Because the wire provides a strong support, the design of a sculpture like this daisy-sniffing dinosaur is limited only by one's imagination, and the time and materials available.

Figure B: To make a garment that can be used to dress any puppet, start with a piece of fabric measuring about 16 by 11 inches. With right sides facing, fold the fabric in half to make an 8-by-11-inch rectangle. Sew the sides together, making ¼-inch seams. Leave an opening for the puppet's hands (or the puppeteer's fingers) on each side near the folded edge. Slash an opening for the neck, and turn the garment right side out.

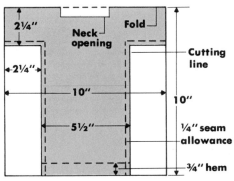

Figure C: To make a shirt-like garment, start with a piece of fabric approximately 10 by 20 inches. (Be sure the finished garment will cover your hand and wrist.) Right sides facing, fold the fabric in half to make a 10-by-10-inch square, and cut out the shirt, following the measurements in the drawing above. Sew the sides, making ¼-inch seams. Turn up the hem and sew it. Turn the garment right side out, and cut the neck opening.

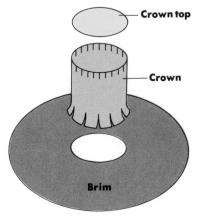

Figure D: To assemble a cowboy hat from the three parts sketched, cut ½-inch-deep slits ½ inch apart along the bottom edge of the crown, and cut ¼-inch-deep slits ¼ inch apart along the top edge. The crown is a cylinder with ends overlapped ½ inch and held with tape. Bend the bottom tabs outward and glue to the brim. Bend the top tabs inward and glue to the crown top.

Materials

For this project, you will need: papier-mâché pulp and strips (Craftnotes, page 1402); dry newspaper; No. 14 galvanized wire; wire cutter; sandpaper or file (available in hardware stores); masking tape; water-base paint such as poster paint or acrylic; white glue; paint brush; scissors; the sculpture may be displayed on a base such as a wood block (optional). The figure may be decorated with artificial flowers, fabric and yarn scraps, and brightly colored paper freckles cut with a paper punch.

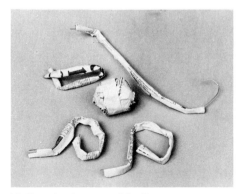 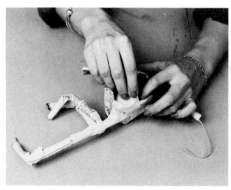 

10: To make the parts of the dinosaur armature, wrap lengths of wire with dry newspaper and curve them into shape. Before bending, the spine (top) was 18 inches long; the arm unit (top left), 12 inches long; and each leg (bottom) was 10 inches long. The body is a ball of dry newspaper (center).

11: Tape the parts of the armature together, making a skeleton for your figure. Adjustments in the design should be made at this point. Since this is a fantasy figure, it need not have realistic proportions, but it should capture an interesting pose. Props may be taped to the figure at this point.

12: Cover the armature with several layers of paper strips, gradually building up the form of the dinosaur. Smooth each strip as it is applied, and fill in gaps between the parts with wads of newspaper or ropes made of twisted newspaper strips which have been soaked in the paste solution.

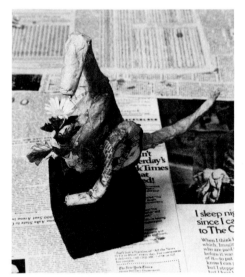

13: Before the papier-mâché is dry, place the figure on a flat surface or on the base you intend to use. At this stage, the model will still be pliable enough so you can make any changes necessary to make it sit or stand as you planned.

Making the Armature

This armature consists of four pieces of wire wrapped in dry newspaper—two separate leg wires, one wire for the arms that are attached at the shoulder, and a wire for the spine (which includes both head and tail). Refer to photograph 10 when you make these parts. The body is a crumpled wad of dry newspaper wrapped with strips of masking tape. To make the limbs and the spine, cut a piece of wire the right length, and tape dry newspaper around it loosely to thicken it. Then bend the wire into shape. This lays the groundwork for the finished figure. In the armature for the dinosaur, the tip of the tail is left unwrapped to let it taper to a point in the finished figure. A bit of wire is also left exposed at the head end; it will support the tongue. The next step is to tape the parts together (photograph 11); the armature should resemble a stick figure and be on the slim side.

Applying Papier-Mâché

Cover the work surface with sheets of newspaper and a layer of waxed paper. Put papier-mâché strips on the armature (photograph 12) to hold the parts together; then build up the figure. If you have added any props (such as the flowers I used), be careful not to get any paste on them. Test the stability of the figure while it is still wet and pliable (photograph 13). Let the figure dry (the Craftnotes on page 1405 tell how to speed drying). If the shrinkage has been severe, dampen the surface with water and add more strips. You can also use pulp to compensate for shrinkage, and to refine the surface. Apply pulp in thin layers with your fingers and build up the form gradually. The dinosaur's ears are folded pieces of cardboard attached with a bit of paper pulp. Spikes are paper strips snaking along the spine; they were allowed to dry and then were trimmed with scissors. Let the figure dry and smooth the surface with a file or sandpaper if you wish.

Painting and Decorating

Paint the figure, using as many coats as needed to obliterate the newsprint. You can paint on a design or leave the figure a solid color and paste on bits of paper or fabric for decoration. Place the figure on the base, and glue in place.

For related crafts and projects, see "Casting," "Molding Methods," "Puppetry," and "Sculpture."